Praise for *Secrets of Santa Muerte*

"I really appreciate Cressida's point of view on Santa Muerte, and I like the way she writes about our spirituality. I hope everyone will like this book that is derived from the writer's lived experiences and shares so much about our people and our rich traditions. I wish Cressida Stone every success."

—Arely Vázquez, leader of Santa Muerte, Queens, New York

"I very rarely endorse nonacademic books, but this grimoire by Cressida Stone is, hands down, the very best and most complete of the spiritual guides on devotion to Santa Muerte, the fastest-growing new religious movement in the West. *Secrets of Santa Muerte* is grounded in the prayers, rituals, and spells developed in Mexico where Holy Death originated. Unlike so many other grimoires and even some academic texts, this devotional road map features the Lady of the Shadows in every single one of her cloaks of many colors—red for love and lust, gold for prosperity and abundance—and even relates how Mexican devotees combine colors for added potency. Penned in captivating prose that engages the reader on every page, Stone's grimoire belongs on the top shelf of both neophytes and seasoned devotees seeking to develop their relationship with the Bone Mother."

—Dr. R. Andrew Chesnut, author of *Devoted to
Death: Santa Muerte, the Skeleton Saint*

"I am pleased to endorse the publication of *Secrets of Santa Muerte* by Cressida Stone. This publication is a well-written book about a belief system that is found in Mexico, as well as many parts of the US. The history, prayers, rituals, etc. of la Santa Muerte offer information that many will enjoy."

—Dr. Eliseo Torres, professor of traditional medicine
courses at the University of New Mexico

"Cressida Stone is an incredible writer who is very intelligent and knows a lot about Santa Muerte; she goes into the fine details very well. I admire her as a woman and as a writer who is dedicated to explaining, with great clarity and without hiding anything, the themes pertaining to Santa Muerte. Her words transmit light, darkness, healing, power, happiness and gratitude."

—Soraya Arredondo Hernandez, *bruja, curandera,*
founder, and leader of *Templo Altar Angel de Alas Negras*
(Angel of Black Wings Temple Altar), Tula, Hidalgo, Mexico

"I confirm and attest that Cressida Stone has deep knowledge of the spirituality of Santa Muerte. She has traveled across Mexico where the roots of devotion to the Saint of Death truly originate. She honors our faith and shares the teachings of Santa Muerte clearly, aiding people to respectfully venerate and learn correctly about

Santisima Muerte. This is because Cressida has been to those special places where devotion to Holy Death is deep and true."

—Yuri Mendez, Bruja of the Three Virtues and spiritual guide of Santa Muerte, leader of the *Templo y Recinto de Sanación Dulce Madre*, Cancún, Quintana Roo, Mexico

"*Secrets of Santa Muerte* offers an insightful look at a culture that I feel many outsiders do not understand or know about, yet feel a great attraction to learning about. This book reveals a series of mysteries, secrets, traditions, beliefs, culture, magic, and spells deeply linked to this ideological current, especially the myth of "the White Girl." In this culture, magic is powerful, raw and real, as is Santa Muerte. We know that, just as light is born in darkness, death gives way to life. Living is arriving; dying is returning; and returning is continuing. This is the eternal lesson of the Santa Muerte."

—Martha Ileana Moran Gonzalez, founder and director of Witchmart, high priestess, and proud *bruja*

"*Secrets of Santa Muerte* is the most complete workbook I have found in English on this subject. After reading it, you will be well equipped to navigate the botanica for supplies and have a solid understanding of how to use those supplies in your spells and witchcraft. Stone goes beyond the well-known color systems and reveals the secrets of lesser-known powders, oils, and candles, and how they are used. There is even a chapter on unbonding with Santa Muerte, for those who decide the faith is not for them and want to respectfully stop working with her. Anyone interested in the fastest growing religious movement in the world should have this book on their shelf."

—Jason Miller, author of *Consorting with Spirits*

"Cressida Stone's *Secrets of Santa Muerte* is the Santa Muerte book we've all been waiting for: a brave blood and guts master class in how best to bond with the Queen of Death. Part personal journey and part history, it focuses mainly on how to work with the Bony Lady. The author is no spiritual tourist, trying Santa Muerte on for size, but the real deal, dedicated to The Lady of the Shadows, and she writes with the authority of both humble seeker and sincere teacher. Stone gives careful advice on how and why to set up an altar including details about herbs, candles, and omens, as well as sharing what she has learned, first hand, from shamans and healers and devotees in Mexico. One of my favorite parts of the book—and I have many—is when Stone describes the ritual of the blood pact, recommended to her by a mountain-dwelling witch. But you'll have to read the book for the whole story! My one wish is that Stone decides to write a companion volume, as the power and beauty of Holy Death in concert with Stone's knowledge and passion made me hungry for more. If you are curious about Santa Muerte or want to deepen your devotion to her, then you need this book."

—Aliza Einhorn, author of *The Little Book of Saturn* and *A Mystical Practical Guide to Magic*

Secrets of
Santa Muerte

A Guide to the Prayers, Spells, Rituals, and Hexes

CRESSIDA STONE

WEISER
BOOKS

This edition first published in 2022 by Weiser Books, an imprint of

Red Wheel/Weiser, LLC
With offices at:
65 Parker Street, Suite 7
Newburyport, MA 01950
www.redwheelweiser.com

ISBN: 978-1-57863-772-0

Library of Congress Cataloging-in-Publication Data available upon request.

Cover design by Kathryn Sky-Peck
Interior by Steve Amarillo / Urban Design LLC
Typeset in Caslon Pro and Antique

Printed in the United States of America

IBI

10 9 8 7 6 5 4 3 2 1

This book is dedicated to the many witches, healers, shamans, and devotees who taught me the ways of Holy Death and opened their hearts and homes to me, but above all it is dedicated to the most beautiful and sacred Santísima Muerte, whom I thank for all the many blessings both material and immaterial, for the innumerable wonders, and many magical moments. May she always protect me and grant me with mystic insights and abundance in all aspects until the last day and ultimate hour when forever I will find rest within her most tender, bony embrace.

AUTHOR NOTE

In this book, the word *Death*, indicating a mystical figure—a personage—is capitalized to distinguish it from *death*, indicating the regular noun meaning the termination of life.

Contents

Preface

I am an occultist; perhaps it is the varied hues of my life that led me to the mysteries. As a child, I was born in a country that was different from my national origins. My family, due to my father's job, shifted around from place to place, never settling, encountering new languages and new spiritual traditions in every new locale. I never truly had a home. I never had a place I felt at peace in. I was ever anticipating the next move, the next language to learn, the next stepping stone, the next space I was supposed to call home but that would be just another pebble in the path of life.

As an adult, I have spent my life traveling the world. I choose to live off the grid as much as possible, to distance myself from the fleeting and superfluous and, instead, to learn and record spiritual traditions from across the globe. It is in spiritual rites that I find tranquility and meaning, a space outside the vicissitudes and vagaries of life. I have traveled to Europe, China, India, the Middle East, Africa, and more recently Latin America, working closely with religious practitioners to learn spiritual traditions from Vodun to Santa Muerte.

I find myself drawn to those traditions that are the most secretive, wherein I swim in the sacred and flow into moments of profound prayer and deep, pensive ritual. Through friendships and deep bonds with advanced practitioners, who, like me, seek only the spiritual, I unlock mysteries and breathe in the bliss of occult obscurities. There are spiritual forces at play in our universe. It is up to the individual to open up these gates, and step into their wonders to live more fully, freely, and more powerfully in sync with the divine.

Nevertheless, having encountered myriad majestic deities and spiritualities, moving from place to place, exploring one and then another, looking for a space that felt like home, where I might at long last feel free and full, only one has drawn me in so deeply I find I must dedicate my days and nights to her forever. Death herself has become my life. Holy Death is the one and only constant. Her bony hands always offer me a place of refuge where, beneath her scythe, I may humbly swim in her sumptuous sacrality and be whole with all. I invite you to join me, dear reader, as I take you on a journey, not only peppered with a few personal anecdotes but, above all, replete with accurate information I have spent years collating to teach you the ways of Santa Muerte. This voyage will open the door to Death and her powers, if you are ready, willing, and able to step into her portal, to let go of fear and to embrace the ultimate truth. She can heal, help, hex, and much more. If, with humility, you respect her great potency and absolute mystery, then perhaps you, like me, will find the place of peace, power, and above all, the sacred sphere you have long been looking for.

· · · · · ❈ · · · · ·

I was living in Mexico when one night, on a full moon, I had a near-death experience. I literally stared death in the face when my car crashed off a ridge. I survived miraculously with zero injuries. As I walked away from the wreck, I realized that my accident had taken place right by a shrine to Santa Muerte. I knew it was a sign. I walked up the ridge into the chapel and, for the second time that night, stared death in the face. Santa Muerte smiled at me. She had just saved my life. I had shivers running down my spine. In a moment of déjà vu, I knew that I had been there before and that I was exactly where I was supposed to be. As I stood in the chapel, a witch of Santa Muerte emerged suddenly from the shadows. Smiling, with mystery twinkling in her dark eyes, I felt death had come to me again, to talk to me. The *bruja* (witch) told me she had been sent by Santa Muerte. She was expecting me; Holy Death told her I would be there that night. Santa Muerte came to her in a dream and said she would send an owl as a sign I had arrived. That very night, an owl had perched itself outside her dwelling, and she knew it was time. We spoke at length that night about the power of death. Everything began to change in my life from that moment on. She introduced me into the community of those who work with death. I met devotees, *brujos*, healers, as well as devotional leaders, not only in Veracruz, where my crash occurred, but across the country.

As the days advanced, Santa Muerte nurtured me, keeping me safe even in the most dangerous areas of Mexico where my deathly research led me. She delivered miracles and magic moments that proved so remarkable that worship of death suffused my soul without even my realizing it. I began to dream of Death and to make profound connections in the Santa Muerte community across Mexico, to holy healers and magic workers, and to devotees. The importance of their knowledge became clear to me. As we engaged in rituals, rosaries, and conversations, and enjoyed meals together, they told me that they wished this knowledge to be recorded and transmitted for future generations and for people outside of Mexico to know the true ways of la Santa Muerte and the path of Death.

One night, again on a full moon, nine months later, I had a thanatophanic dream of Death herself.[1] Santa Muerte appeared to me in a glimmering gown of purest purple with a moonshine-silver sash around her waist and whispered to me in the way that only Death can, a sound so unique I will never forget the chills it sent down my spine. I was tasked by her to honor her name by writing a book dedicated to her, not so much about my journey, but rather to teach others about her miraculous powers and magical wonders. It is my calling to share these lessons with those seeking, like me, to dive deep into the mysteries of life and death.

I have seen so much misinformation about the Powerful Lady (as she is often known in Mexico) and misconceptions, whether accusations of her satanic nature or total miscomprehension of practices and beliefs outside of Mexico. Through the guiding bony hand of Santa Muerte, always following her directions, as well as with the aid of practitioners in Mexico, I penned this book for neophytes, advanced practitioners, and spiritual seekers who wish to know Death and her force in all creation, as well as expiration.

---

1 A theophanic vision is one of God (*theo* in Greek), appearance (*phany*). In this context, a thanatophanic dream is the appearance of death (*thanatos*). *Thanatos* comes from the Greek, meaning the personification of death.

In Santa Muerte spirituality, as I have seen in Mexico, there is ultimately much flexibility, and varied viewpoints exist on many matters. Judgment is seldom cast, from those within the folk faith, on the way in which people practice their devotion to this female folk saint, and it is understood, especially in places of poverty, that sumptuous offerings cannot always be given, that sometimes only a plain, cheap white candle can be lit, rather than a special Santa Muerte votive, as this is all you can afford. And Santa Muerte will understand this, if this is all you have, but as I will explain, an abundance of faith is critical. Despite heteropraxy, there are key practices and concepts that are essential to this folk faith. This book outlines these key tenets. They should serve as a starting point for any nascent practitioner.

The book features some prayers that are widely used across Mexico. All are authentic, deriving only from Mexican sources, so I have translated them from Spanish. Where possible, when rhymes featured in the original Spanish, I have attempted to retain such lyricism while preserving the meaning as close as possible to the original. This book features many ancient and key prayers, such as the ubiquitous Novena (nine-day prayer) "Return a Wayward Lover" and others that have been used across Mexico and featured on prayer cards to Santa Muerte since at least the 1940s, but are no doubt far older. It also features prayers that are not ubiquitous but that I have collected from witches and shamans from across Mexico. Prayer is vital, indeed far more so than the size or opulence of your altar. Prayer is the key to opening communication with Santa Muerte.

If your altar is simple, your statue is small, or even homemade, that is not a problem. If your candle is only of a generic kind and not a specific Santa Muerte–emblazoned candle, this does not mean that your prayers will be ignored. In Mexico, where poverty is widespread and resources scarce, people practice with what they can, when they can, and how they can. One thing the marvelous devotees of Mexico have taught me is that all practice and prayer must be infused with effort, utmost respect, total faith, and deep spirituality. What most Mexican devotees of Santa Muerte sadly lack in material goods (due to gross inequalities caused by government corruption, drug wars, and greed), they make up for with their kindness and patience in explaining their beliefs, as I have been fortunate enough to experience and, most of all, their profound faith.

That is the lesson I have taken away more than any other, and that I impart to you, dear reader, and if you take one thing away from this book, it must be this: *the importance of regular prayer, deep devotion, and absolute faith.* I have seen such fervent, unwavering reverence and profound dedication to Death in Mexico. Indeed, the intensity of faith is of a depth that I have seldom seen elsewhere during my travels across the world. Therefore, this book, while dedicated to la Santa Muerte, is also written in homage to the Mexican people who are deeply devoted to Death. They taught me what true spirituality is, the value of prayer, of patience and willingness to wait for Santa Muerte to come through. They taught me to understand that as we tread this path, we will meet both life and death, light and dark, and that we must embrace both, not in fear, no matter how hard that may be, but uncomplainingly and patiently, knowing that Santa Muerte will guide us, even on the darkest night, and if it is into her arms, *que así sea*, so be it. Darkness is part of life, as is death, and balances out light and life. Each is necessary to the other and indeed part of the other, and you must learn this no matter how hard that lesson is. It is part of Santa Muerte's message. Every evening when I go to sleep, I understand that she may take me, but every day she lets me live, every moment she gifts me another breath, I am grateful to her and, above all, for keeping those I love alive. The ones who are no longer living, I know are in her embrace, and so I pray for the living and the dead to Death. Prayer is a portal to her holiness. Prayer must be any dedicated devotees' life and *death-bread.*

Mexican devotees of the folk saint of death instilled in me the knowledge that regular, committed, and unwavering devotion is crucial, whether in good, bad, or ugly times, whether in darkness or in light. I thank Santa Muerte from the bottom of my heart and soul for all she has shown me, given me, taught me, blessed me with, as well as the many devotees, *curanderos,* and *brujos* who guided me, kept me safe and sound, and taught me the secrets of the Lady of the Shadows. I will hold your life and death lessons in my heart till Death do us reunite and I am merged with her forever in the darkness and light of the thanatic eternities.

CHAPTER ONE

Who Is Santa Muerte and Why Work with Her?

Cressida Stone

Introduction

Santa Muerte is the powerful and mystical Mexican female folk saint of death. She is depicted as a female Grim Reaper. Although she may be portrayed in many ways, in most iconography she wears a long gown tied with a sash at her waist. A mantle covers her bare skull. In her skeletal right hand, she wields a scythe. In her bony left hand, she holds a globe or the scales of justice. She is often accompanied by an owl, her messenger and companion animal. In her home country of Mexico, millions pray to her, for she is supremely mighty and an effective miracle worker who gifts magical wonders and blessings of all kinds to those who worship her devoutly. She has a formidable persona and a multifaceted character, as you will learn as you get to know her.

While she is caring, motherly, and generous with her devotees, Santa Muerte is also vindictive or wrathful to those who do not come through on their promises to her, who disrespect her, or who insult and disrespect her children, her loyal devotees. She is very open-minded and will listen to anyone who prays to her—that is, if they treat her properly with the deference she deserves. She has even punished me along my journey with her. Once, I was at her altar pouring out some mezcal for myself and la Santa Muerte. Lacking deference, I drank my mezcal first before placing her glass before her. She was livid! The next thing I knew the bottle of booze had fallen off the shelf and half its contents had flowed out onto the floor. But Santa Muerte, if you give her the love, devotion, and attention she deserves, is wonderfully generous. Santísima Muerte has saved my life more than once, healed me from deep illness, aided me financially, and protected me from evil many times. She has safeguarded my loved ones and given me opportunities I could never have dreamt of, both in the realms of the sacred and the profane. Holy Death is deeply profound and mystical; therefore, she can gift you with knowledge and insights through visions and dreams. If you learn to listen to the signs, she will forewarn you of danger, as she has me. At the same time, for all her otherworldliness, Santa Muerte is not only Queen of Death but also a maiden of merriment who enjoys what this world has to offer. She relishes fine food, drink, sometimes a smoke, and even a party held in her honor. This is why her altar should never be bare.

Santa means "saint" or "holy" in Spanish, while *muerte* means "death." Santa Muerte is therefore the folk saint of death; she channels the awesome and holy power that is death. As a devotee, you may also call her, as is done in Mexico, *Santísima Muerte*, which means "Most Holy Death." You may choose to use her English name as some devotees do in the US and UK, calling her *Saint Death* or *Holy Death*. In this book, I also use the English translation to remind readers who do not speak Spanish that Santa Muerte is not an abstract name and that they must learn to tap into the power of Death.

As shamans, who are known as *curanderas* (female form) or *curanderos* (male form; also used as the plural encompassing both male and female shamans) told me across Mexico, death is the most powerful force in the universe, since death comes to all of us. No one can escape Santa Muerte's bony clutches when their death knell rings. Death is therefore the ultimate truth and the strongest force that unites us all. Death is supreme. Santa Muerte is this power of death in the form of a female saint who is timeless, ageless, and accessible to all who find her and learn to respect and work with her properly.

Santa Muerte is an unofficial (not canonized) saint, one unrecognized by the Catholic Church and whom Mexicans have long channeled as a spiritual power as I describe in the next chapter on her history. The Catholic Church is critical of her, despite the fact that many devotees see themselves as Catholic. I have no doubt that this is due to the Church's dwindling power and hold in the region. For them, Santa Muerte is a threat.

When the loyal practitioner prays to Holy Death, honors her, bonds with her, and otherwise learns to work with her, she will offer many miracles and empower *brujeria* (magic work), gifting healing, riches, good luck, love, protection, and numerous other wonders. When you start researching Santa Muerte, you will discover that her images, statues, and candles come in many colors. Each hue represents a distinct aspect of her persona and powers, so to be a knowledgeable practitioner, you must learn these color schemes as there is a vast contrast in the work, in the interactions you have with her, and the outcomes, depending on what color Santa Muerte you devote yourself to and work with. Powders, oils, and herbs empower *brujeria* and prayers, as I detail. Insect and animal omens and symbols may be used to divine the future and glean insights into the present, as I describe. Death does not judge, as she comes to us all, whether nurse, housewife, musician, criminal, lawyer, police officer, teacher, doctor, boxer, bus driver, or someone who uses drugs; we are all equal before death. Therefore, you can ask Santa Muerte for favors of all kinds, even those you might not wish to ask a spirit or saint whom you think is judgmental. Death listens to *anyone*. As I was told, for all of us, no matter who we are, *"La vida solamente es un paso a la Muerte"* (Life is only a path to death.).

It does not matter your color, your age, your origins, your class status, your sexuality, your lifestyle choices, or your nationality. As I was told time and time again in Mexico, Death comes for us all. There is no one who cannot work with her—only immortals! Having said this, you invite Death into your life when you work with her, and you must be aware that she is a potent force. She may test the strength of your devotion with hurdles to see whether you are seriously devoted. She has tested me and many of those I love who are devotees. If she does not think you are devoted, respectful, or ready, she will not respond to you. Although Death comes to everyone, not everyone can work with her. This work requires devotion, commitment, and the ability to channel and flow with the esoteric, thanatic forces at work in this cosmos. Although this book can guide you on how to do this, only you can open Death's door through deep devotion so as to be blessed with her incredible gifts and wonders. To experience her total power takes time.

In her original form, Santa Muerte is associated with the colors white, black, and red. These colors represent her primary aspects and the powers for which devotees, *curanderos*, and *brujo*s in Mexico turn to her. All three are vital to practice.

* In her white gown, Santa Muerte is caring and maternal, and she gifts great blessings of health, cleansing, and well-being.

* In her black manifestation, Santísima Muerte is powerful, vengeful, and formidable. Turn to her, not only for malevolent magic but also strength and protection.

* Dressed in red robes, she is beguiling, playful, and passionate. Love and lust magic are her specialty. She can help you find a lover or spouse. As Santa Muerte does not judge, she can also aid you in your sex life, including for same-sex love, as well as all petitions of a sexual nature. As she is powerful, she will help you control situations of all types, including favors of sexual and amorous domination.

This book instructs you on how to work with all three of these key attributes of Santa Muerte. It also teaches you how to use other colors, such as amber, yellow, green, silver, gold, bone, brown, pink and purple; to combine colors; and to use specific Mexican candles to reap financial, spiritual, and intellectual success. You will learn, if you wish to, how to hex others, but also to reverse spells, as well as dispel envy and evil sent your way, so as to open your path and receive Santa Muerte's gifts of abundance.

As long as you are devoted to Most Holy Death, cultivate knowledge of her, respect her, pray regularly, maintain a clean and generous altar to her, and develop a deep, loving relationship, Santa Muerte will listen to any petition you make, and decide whether to honor it. If you have enough faith and follow her guidance, she may come through for you. As I have learned, you may have to be patient; a petition may take time to be heard as the elements fall into place and align in your favor. You need to kindle your bond with Santa Muerte from the tinder of many gestures and prayers, as well as learn to swim in the sacred energy and currents of her profound power. The door to Death will lead you into understanding everything anew.

I have asked *curanderos* why some petitions are not heard. I impart their wisdom to you. They told me: either because the supplication's outcomes are deemed inappropriate for you, or the timing is wrong, or your relationship with and faith in Santa Muerte is not sufficient and you are not truly devoted, or perhaps you need patience and things will change. Importantly, dear reader, you should know that Santa Muerte sometimes works in mysterious and unexpected ways. I have sometimes petitioned her for something I wanted, only for a seemingly bad event to happen the next day. But a few weeks later, I noted that the unwanted event turned out to be good for me, to be her way of protecting me from a dire danger that would have harmed me. Nevertheless, Santa Muerte will come through for you if this is in your interests. She is, above all other saints, whether official or folk saint, known to be an efficient and fast-acting miracle worker. Notwithstanding, the Saint of Death, as witches will tell you in Mexico, is not only immensely powerful but also vengeful and fickle; therefore, you must work with her respectfully and keep the promises you make to her, or she may punish you. This book will teach you how to work respectfully and effectively with Santa Muerte and tap into the powerful force that is Death herself.

In the US and Western Europe, we have learned to fear death, but as shamans taught me in Mexico, death is the key to all life and to creation. As I was told repeatedly, in Mexican traditional thought and Indigenous understandings, life and death are in a perpetual cycle, and each nourishes the other. Death is a creative force that can breathe power and success into any aspect of your life. Death is not something to fear but to embrace, not only to prepare yourself for your inevitable passing and that of others, but also because if worked with properly, the power of Death can infuse life and luck into all your undertakings, from love to business affairs. This is why Santa Muerte, often known as the Powerful Lady because of her potency, must be treated with respect and reverence.

Holy Death is easy to identify, as she often wields a large scythe, and you may find her statue online or in botanicas (stores that sell religious paraphernalia) in the US and elsewhere. But do not confuse her with la Catrina, who has no spiritual power and is erroneously bought by non-Mexican neophytes in her stead. La Catrina is a satirical figure of death as a dame, often in a large, floppy hat, who originated from the pen of José Posada as a social critique of government corruption in the 1900s. She appears in Day of the Dead festivities and generally looks a lot more frivolous and girly than Santa Muerte.

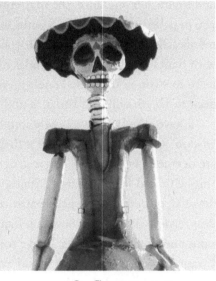

pixabay.com

La Catrina

It is crucial to obtain an image or Santa Muerte statue in order to work with her, whether it is a printed image, a home-made statue, or a purchased effigy. It is vital that rituals should be undertaken to awaken and activate the image or statue. The effigies you buy need not be large, elaborate, or expensive, and for the thrifty practitioner starting out, a printed image of the saint suffices, although it is recommended that a statue be made or obtained eventually. What is key is to perform a ritual and possibly name your image/statue so that she bonds with you and Santa Muerte's spirit can work through the effigy.

Some creative devotees outside of Mexico buy skeletons in craft stores and sew, design, and bead their own gowns for her. In Mexico, those who work with wood or other artisanal methods carve and create their own unique statues in honor to her. Wood is an ideal element to use in creating Santa Muerte effigies, as you will learn in chapter four. Feel free to create your own Santa Muerte effigy if you have such skills; however, if you make your own statue, remember to keep with the materials and color themes for the petitions you seek and to give her the accoutrements with which she is typically depicted, as described in this book.

Overall, statues are strongly recommended and will help you forge a relationship with Santa Muerte as she is embodied in her statue. She can be appealed to, communicated with through her statue, which will take on her spirit. It is important to pay attention to whether her statue seems content and to observe goings-on around her. This will give you an indication of her mood. If things fall around her, or she seems angry, you will need to attend to her. You must see if something such as an old or unwanted offering is upsetting her and remove it, or perhaps clean her altar if you have not

done so in a while. The procedure for doing this is outlined in chapter three; it teaches you how to remove negative energy from your altar which could sabotage your spell work.

Cressida Stone

Images of the saint can be found on specific, different-colored votive candles, which are an essential part of practicing the Santa Muerte faith and petitioning her for favors. Devotees also purchase and wear medallions or bracelets or carry prayer cards featuring her image with them when they are on the go, for protection and luck. Small, pocket-sized statues may be

Who Is Santa Muerte and Why Work with Her?

carried as needed for luck, while you are away from home, perhaps at a court hearing, on a dangerous journey, or even on a date for the purposes of love and sex sorcery. It is recommended that these objects be cleaned and purified with herbal water, possibly tobacco smoke, and incense regularly to ensure that the negative energy they absorb is removed. This book teaches you how to do this. Santa Muerte likes to be kept clean. A sloppy altar or dusty pendant will attract misfortune, as she will take out her anger on the devotee who ignores her desire for being bathed and adored.

Imagery

Santa Muerte is consistently represented as a female Grim Reaper on all paraphernalia, from candles to pendants and beyond. Easily recognizable, she has a skull for a head, hollow eyes, and usually wears a long gown down to her skeletal toes. Santa Muerte typically carries a scythe in her right hand. In her bony left hand, she generally carries a globe or the scales of justice, and at her feet is an owl. Sometimes devotees, as you will learn, remove her scythe from her right hand to place special prayers in that hand, especially during *brujeria*.

While death in the United States is often personified as male, it is crucial to remember that in Mexico, Santa Muerte is first and foremost female. *Curanderos*, witches, and devotees perceive her as a mother who protects them, and who may punish them or their enemies, although sometimes they also see her as a capricious girl. They call her both *Madre* (mother) and *Niña* (girl), *la Flaquita* (the skinny girl), *Madrina* (godmother), and other terms of endearment. Yet, no matter how they refer to her—and she boasts many names—she is considered to be female and highly powerful and may even be called *Dominadora* (she who dominates: a dominatrix) or *Reina* (Queen), referring to her supreme power. It is therefore important to treat her as a thanatic monarch, as she is the Queen of Death.

Some of the many names used to refer to Santa Muerte follow:

* *La Niña Bonita:* The Pretty Girl

* *La Madrina:* The Godmother

* *La Flaquita:* The Skinny Girl

* *La Huesuda:* The Bony Lady

* *La Hermana Blanca:* The White Sister

* *La Dama Poderosa:* The Powerful Lady

* *La Niña Blanca:* The White Girl (this refers to her in her white form but may also mean Santa Muerte in general)

* *La Niña Negra:* The Black Girl; this always refers to her ebony form

* *La Dama de las Sombras:* The Lady of the Shadows

As she is Queen of Death, some devotees adorn her with tiaras and crowns and jewels as well as other opulent accoutrements, which you may also choose to do. Remember to spoil her with gifts, especially when seeking her support in spiritual matters. In particular, she is known for her fondness for flowers, alongside other gifts. Devotees in Mexico told me that she loves roses, carnations, irises, and lilies. The Mexican flower of death, *cempasuchil,* or the marigold *(Tagetes spp.)* should be offered to her in November, or even yearlong. The color of the flowers you gift her should correspond with the favors you seek from her.

I recommend you gift flowers, food, and alcohol, too, as regularly as you can. This is essential when you are asking for her help with a matter. Change the water of these flowers regularly to keep them fresh. You must be generous with her after she has made good on a request you made of her. In Mexico, I never visited a Santa Muerte shrine or the altar of a *curandero* with empty hands. I always brought flowers with me or fruits, and sometimes a bottle of some hard liquor. To not do so would be to disrespect Holy Death. I have heard many a tale of devotees who promised the Pretty Girl flowers or other treats if she came through on a petition they asked her for. However, they forgot or did not bother and were then punished, whether with accidents, a broken heart, bad business matters, or some other unfortunate event. You cannot ignore Death or break a pact with her, for she will come looking for what she is owed.

Santa Muerte is frequently depicted carrying the scales of justice, which symbolizes her potent power in bestowing justice when you most need it. If you are having legal troubles or have been wronged, you can ask the Powerful Lady for equity. Also, since Santa Muerte is not judgmental, justice is whatever you define it as. It is not clear-cut as we often portray it in the US and Western Europe. Justice is whatever your own view is on matters. Therefore, even if you are cognizant that you made a mistake but still do not want to be prosecuted for a transgression, explain this to Santa Muerte. If you honor her and explain your situation, she may listen to you and deliver whatever justice is for you. This is why with Santa Muerte, as will be explained, you can work with both hands: what occultists call the right-hand and left-hand paths. Ideally, however—as recommended to me by Mexican witches in possession of secret knowledge—light and dark forces are best when in balance. You should not veer to one extreme, overly embracing dark *brujeria* and wishing harm on people too frequently or indiscriminately.

When Santa Muerte carries the scales of justice, it is also a warning not to delve too deeply into the darkness, as she watches her devotees closely and keeps her own balance. I have heard tales of narcos and *brujos* too deeply invested in la Niña Negra. They performed blood sacrifices and routinely wished evil upon their enemies but eventually had to pay back the Lady of the Shadows for all the harm she had granted them. One such witch wished the annihilation of many people, from neighbors to coworkers, and, ultimately, death violently visited her beloved boyfriend. One night, the two of them were supposed to meet for a romantic dinner, but he never arrived. On his way, his vehicle's brakes failed, and his car spun off the highway, crashing into the rocks by the road and smashing into a million pieces. I also heard of a narco, known to visit the shrine near my lodgings in the dead of night, to work *hechicerias* (sorceries) of the most nefarious kind on his enemies. He had asked for so much harm that one day Death came calling for payback for all the lives lost due to his acts. His daughter died. She was five years old. She fell into a swimming pool while playing and drowned. While natural death in Mexico is considered part of the normal cycle of life, Mexicans also recognize what they call *mala muerte*, that is to say "bad death." This is when someone dies young, or unexpectedly, and in tragic circumstances. In Mexico, it is said that Santa Muerte may bring *mala muerte* to your door if you work incorrectly and too vindictively. This is therefore a warning, both literally and spiritually: tread lightly into the dark side. When you do, pay what you owe. Be aware that there are consequences, and when you deal with Death to bring death to others, your own life, and that of those you love, is also on the scales that Holy Death holds. She can tip them at any time.

Santa Muerte's iconography aligns with her powers, which the practitioner should tap into through her. As we have seen, the scales of justice depict her power to support you in legal matters and to get retribution. If you seek her help in such matters, I recommend that you obtain an effigy with the scales in her hand and robed in the color that best suits your needs:

* Green, the color of justice

* Black, should you also need protection, and potentially revenge

* White, should you need cleansing, healing, peace, and harmony

* Garbed in her seven-colored cloak if you need things to align in perfect synergy for you

These color schemes are discussed further in chapters four and five.

Santa Muerte is also portrayed as carrying a globe. This depiction signifies her power over life and death. This portrays her total dominion of death: her ability to extinguish all life on earth. But it also shows how she is able to infuse new life into ventures and make dreams come true all over the world. Santa Muerte, as ruler over earth and dispenser of death, presides over us all, no matter who we are and where we are. While some outside of Mexico claim that Santa Muerte is a "closed practice" and only for people of Mexican origin, this is not what I was told in Mexico. Devotees from all over Mexico told me repeatedly: we all die; death does not see color, class, nationality, or sexuality; therefore, we are all welcomed to work with the Lady of the Shadows, as long as we respect her, take the time to honor her properly, and learn her secrets. It is not the case that she does not listen to White people; indeed, the late Enriqueta Vargas (who died in 2018 and is now forever in the arms of Santa Muerte) and Adriana Llubere (who calls herself *la güera,* a slang term meaning a white girl, on her YouTube channel and elsewhere) are both powerful—and white-skinned—Santa Muerte leaders. The globe therefore points to her global nature, to the power of death across the world, and that we are all her children, no matter who we are, and we will all die. Since statues of la Santa with the globe signify her power over all earthly endeavors, they are a good choice for those seeking to regain control over matters in their lives.

Santa Muerte is nearly always depicted with a scythe in her right hand. This is an important part of her persona and powers. It not only represents her ability as a psychopomp to reap the souls of the deceased but also symbolizes her force as she who cuts away negative energies and influences. Working with her scythe, you as a practitioner can imagine in your mind's eye—as you carry out the rituals outlined in this book—Santa Muerte cutting away whatever it is you need sliced out from your life. This could be enemies, bad energy, unfavorable weather conditions, gossipers, injustices, envious troublemakers, or illness. For this reason, it is recommended to work with statues that have scythes for clearing away anything unwanted, as some effigies do not have the scythe, especially the smaller ones.

Santa Muerte is often portrayed with an owl at her feet. The owl is her messenger and companion. In Mexico, the owl is associated with both wisdom and death. The old Mexican expression is "When the owl screeches, the Indian dies." Although owls are harbingers of death in Mexico, for devotees of Santa Muerte, if you see an owl, it may also be a good omen that Holy Death is watching over you. The owl depicts death in animal form but also signifies Santa Muerte's wisdom and ability to see—and help you see—clearly. To ensure the bird's power flows through their life, devotees should place additional owls on their altars.

You may petition Santa Muerte and her avian messenger to deliver guidance to you through whatever medium she sees fit to transmit this through. This may be a vision, dream, or secret message for you to interpret. Some devotees use tarot, others use dreams, some use animal omens, and it is up to the individual practitioner to work with whatever medium they deem appropriate to channel her messages. This book will guide you on this aspect, giving you information on ceromancy, which is how to interpret candle wax at the end of burnt candles and candle jars, and animal as well as insect signs to divine the future.

Shamans are not strict about the means of communicating with Holy Death, as I saw in Mexico, and it is important to work with your own abilities and strengths to obtain messages from her. As a practitioner, if you can do this, you will be able to find out hidden knowledge and access esoteric truths thanks to Santa Muerte's crystal-clear vision of all matters of life and death on this earth.

CHAPTER TWO

History of Santa Muerte

Wikimedia Commons

Santa Muerte is a modern version of the power at the heart of an ancient death cult with roots in pre-Hispanic, Indigenous Mexico. *Curanderos* told me that devotion to death is as old as time, as our human species, and its secrets have been imparted in Mexico since we first roamed the earth. We are all mortal. Our knowledge of the power of death is inescapable. The cognizance that our time here on earth will end ultimately with our passing, as will that of all others, means that dying is a vital part of everyone's experience. We may not recall our birth, but we are, especially when faced with difficulties, all conscious that we will die.

In Mexico, among many peoples—from the Aztecs, the Olmec, the Totonacos, the Maya, to the Tarascans—it has always been recognized that life and death are a never-ending cycle and that each powers the other, with death being a precursor to life, fertility, and creation. The Aztec revered Mictecacihuatl, the Goddess of Death and Guardian of Bones who presided over Mictlan, the Underworld, with her husband Mictlantecuhtli. The deathly couple not only reigned over Mictlan, the realm where the dead went after a long journey, but also offered miracles through their power of death to the living. The Aztec and other Indigenous peoples knew how to tune into the power of death to ensure fertile crops, an excellent harvest, to bring life to the wombs of women, and much more. This ancient knowledge has not been forgotten; it still exists today through Santa Muerte.

While some will tell you that Santa Muerte is a recent folk faith that started a few decades ago, the truth is—as explained to me by a Santa Muerte Maya *curandero* who lived deep in the jungle near a *cenote* that few knew about and where he conducted death rituals—that Santa Muerte is both an ancient and modern understanding of the timeless power of death. In the Spanish colony of Mexico, then known as New Spain, devotion to death was driven underground. This happened because Spanish colonizers and their Christian missionaries punished those Indigenous people who worshiped Death with violence and torture. Colonial archives record the details of how Indigenous people were punished for this offense; therefore, we can infer that many have been working with Santa Muerte for centuries. More recently, the Catholic Church's condemnation of Santa Muerte has again caused some people to hide their faith. Indeed, this is why this Maya *curandero* of death preferred to live in the depths of the tropical forest where he could carry out his rituals without judgment, the jungle his herbal apothecary, and the moon his alone.

Santa Muerte spirituality has been hidden away behind closed doors to avoid judgment or punishment and violence for a long time. For decades, devotees have clandestinely kept altars, hidden pendants of Holy Death underneath their shirts, and kept their spiritual practices alive in the privacy of their own homes. One witch told me that she recently found out that her neighbor of thirty years was a devotee. It is only in the last ten years that many have begun to make public their faith and these mysteries have finally come to light.

Although Santa Muerte as the power of Death hails from ancient Indigenous death cults of an antique past, today she is depicted and understood as a mixture of a folk saint and a spirit or goddess belonging to the ancient Mexican death cult. Her hybrid personality and powers come from the era of colonization. When the Spanish came to Mexico in the 1500s to colonize the land, they wanted to convert the local people to Christianity and annihilate ancient Indigenous traditions, which they saw as evil and savage. They brought with them images, statues and stories of Jesus, Mary, Catholic saints, and the Grim Reaper of medieval European Catholicism.

The bubonic plague, also known as the Black Death, was a devastating disease that killed millions of people in 14th-century Europe. During this time, death became personified as the figure known as the Grim Reaper. Painters and priests used the figure to portray the horrors of death and to teach people the necessity of praying to get to heaven while they could, before death grabbed them, lest their sins and lack of prayer entail they be sent to hell. In Spain, the Grim Reaper was a female figure. When Spanish missionaries arrived in Mexico right after the end of the Black Death to aid colonizers in their misguided mission to create what they called "New Spain," they also employed the Grim Reaper, as they had in Europe, to teach the Indigenous peoples about death. This female figure was called *la Parca*. Indigenous peoples had long worshiped death for its great powers.

Instead of seeing the Grim Reaper as a warning to pray to get to heaven when you die, the Indigenous people saw *la Parca* in the light of their own traditions and their knowledge of the power of death, which they wanted to harness. They reconfigured *la Parca* as a sort of Death Goddess.

While the Spanish were busy destroying the Indigenous statues and outlawing Indigenous spiritualities like death cults, it was all the more important for Indigenous peoples to find new, covert ways to continue to honor and pass down their sacred traditions. As a *curandera* explained to me, these were ancient, primal, and immensely powerful forces. Indigenous peoples were not going to just throw them out the window because the Spanish told them to worship the Christian god, who after all had died on the cross, proving that Death was omnipotent, even over Jesus.

Indigenous peoples in Mexico began worshiping *la Parca*, who they saw in the guise of their old Death goddesses and gods. This is documented in colonial archives. The people knew they could tap into deathly powers through her to grant them miracles of all kinds. Even if worship of their old thanatic deities was now forbidden by the Spanish, they could maintain sacred traditions and turn to the Grim Reaper to maintain their relationship with the power of Death. This Grim Reaper they called "Santa Muerte," the saint of death. However, when the Spanish missionaries discovered this, as is recorded in colonial archives, the missionaries were angered. They destroyed the statues and images of Santa Muerte that Indigenous people had been working with and punished the local people.

The Spanish colonizers went to great measures to eradicate veneration of this death cult, driving it underground into the penumbra where Santa Muerte became the Lady of the Shadows. But it did not stop these ancient, occult mysteries from surviving. Over centuries, they were passed down across many generations. As time passed and the Indigenous ways and people died out from the activities of the Spanish colonizers whose power and influence grew along with that of their clergy, these practices became increasingly infused with Catholic touches, such as praying the rosary and seeing Santa Muerte as a saint, but the Catholic Church has never accepted Santa Muerte. She is a folk saint who amalgamates both Indigenous, Catholic, and even other influences from Santeria, New

Age, and other religions. While today praxis is more Catholic, we must acknowledge her Indigenous ancestry, and indeed in Indigenous areas of Mexico, the faith is steeped in ancient traditions of working with herbs and portals, as I have seen.

Many shamans and witches in Mexico are women, who are the keepers of esoteric family knowledge and pass such traditions down to their daughters or aunts to their nieces or grandmothers to their granddaughters; some women passed them to their sons, who then passed them to their children. One such person is Enriqueta Romero, known as Doña Queta. She lives in the rough barrio of Tepito in Mexico City, where she established the first known and now famous public shrine to Santa Muerte.

As a teenager, Doña Queta was called to worship the folk saint. Her aunt had a Santa Muerte altar in the living room and taught her the traditions. After her marriage, Doña Queta set up a small altar in her own kitchen, where she sold quesadillas to her neighbors. Many, seeing the altar, began leaving offerings until they overcrowded the kitchen, and the innumerable candles, some toppling, started a dangerous fire one day.

Doña Queta's son was incarcerated for a crime that his mother has never revealed to me. She told him to pray to Santa Muerte and also petitioned Holy Death to let him be released from the dangerous jail, full of drugs, shanks, and enemies. In 2001, he was freed after Santa Muerte granted Doña Queta the miracle of justice for him. To celebrate, she decided to set her altar outside on Day of the Dead, 2001. The shrine became famous. Countless devotees began to visit. This also led to numerous clandestine devotees bringing their skeletons out of the closet and going public about their devotion to death. Everyone from witches to *curanderos* began working far more openly with Santísima Muerte. But some, as I know, still work in the shadows, preferring to keep their devotion covert.

It should be noted that although Enriqueta's story is the most famous, many other important Santa Muerte leaders also began to work openly with Saint Death around this time. I also acknowledge those who taught me so much, many of whom work in the darkness of the shadows, where their secrets can be best kept and for whom only the deathly gaze of Santa Muerte is necessary. Many public leaders are men, but even more are women. For female practitioners, Most Holy Death is an excellent spirit to work with. The skeleton saint relates to followers of all genders, but as a female spirit, she understands the difficulties of women as a mother or sister would. Some call her *la Hermana Blanca* (the White Sister) for this reason. If you're a male practitioner, you may also forge a deep bond with her. You might wish, as devotees and *brujos* in Mexico do, to work with her as if she were a mother figure to you, or a girlfriend, but remember, if you wish to marry her spirit, you must understand that you are betrothed to her and must love and honor her alone, but she will always be independent and will never be yours.

Doña Queta's shrine in Tepito

Courtesy of Cearan McGrath

CHAPTER THREE

Setting Up an Altar to Santa Muerte, Working with It and Cleansing It

Creating an altar to Santa Muerte is a key element to establishing a relationship with her. Without one, you will be unable to proceed, so the first step in working with Santísima Muerte is to dedicate a private, quiet, personal space in your house, apartment, room, or even workplace to her. This will be a space of devotion for yourself and possibly others should you carry out collective rituals with other devotees.

In this place, you will perform rituals and ceremonies, do spell work, give her gifts, say prayers, and connect with her on a deep level. You will need to be undisturbed: to work without intruders or the gaze of onlookers. This place must be quiet so that you can pray without the interruption of loud noises, a television blaring, or guests arriving. As a *curandera* who lived near the Atoyac River in Guerrero explained to me, you must use your intuition to find the right space. You must feel that this space is ready both physically and spiritually to honor the spirit of la Santísima Muerte. It must be special, worthy of her, and ready to welcome her, as you would a loved and powerful being into your life. Think carefully about where this space could be and make sure it is dedicated to her alone. This *curandera* lived on a large, private piece of land. She created her shrine outside, not far from the river's edge from where she collected water for her Santa Muerte, using this *agua* to feed the herbs she grew for her practice, from *Hierba buena* (mint) to chamomile and sage. But we do not all have such a perfect outdoor space.

If you already have an altar or other spiritual space replete with many figurines of other gods and goddesses, you cannot just add Santa Muerte to it. She demands her own space, so you must give this to her. She will not tolerate sharing a space with other spirit entities, and your spells may not work should you place Santa Muerte amid other spirits, gods, and goddesses, especially those from other traditions. In Mexico, shamans generally have a dedicated space to Santa Muerte in their shrines. Nevertheless, some devotees' altars may feature other specific saints, such as Saint Jude (*San Judas Tadeo*), who is very popular in Mexico, and/or Mexican folk saints such as Jesus Malverde. Santa Muerte is known, as I was told, to "get along with them." In fact, Jesus Malverde, Saint Jude, and Santa Muerte are often known as *la Santísima Trinca*, or the Holy Trinity, among devotees in Mexico. Also images of Jesus feature on numerous shrines in Mexico.

Many prayers, as you will learn, also invoke God's or Jesus's power. I have also seen advocations of the Christ Child such as El Niño Doctor, and sometimes la Virgen de Guadalupe on altars. Some devotees have told me that Holy Death allowed them to have San Cipriano on their altar, although I do not recommend this for the neophyte. In cities and states in Mexico where there is a Cuban influence, such as Mexico City and Veracruz, you will find *orishas* (Yoruba spirits of Santeria) alongside Santa Muerte. This is usually for advanced practitioners. No other figures should feature on your altar if you are a novice, only Santa Muerte.

If you insist on placing Jesus Malverde or Saint Jude on your altar, they must occupy a far smaller place so as to honor Santa Muerte's superior power and dominance. For example, at the spiritual space of a *curandero* I visited frequently, he had shrines to many entities, including one altar table covered with candles and innumerable figures from Saint Jude to the Virgin of Guadalupe to Saint Martin of Porres, but he had a separate altar for Santa Muerte that stood apart. It is therefore advised for the neophyte to have only Santa Muerte in your dedicated spiritual space. If, at a later date, you insist on adding Jesus Malverde, San Cipriano, or Saint Jude, you must have her consent and the statues must be smaller than hers, less numerous, and situated below or around la Santa, who must be central on the altar. If in doubt, ask the Powerful Lady and watch for signs of approval or disapproval, such as positive or negative occurrences, sounds, sights, and feelings, especially around the altar space. If you need extra aid at a desperate time, you may have an extra saint as a "visitor" who comes only during the time needed and then returns to their space. But I personally work with la Santa Muerte only on her altar space. After all, she is known in Mexico as *la Patrona* (the boss) and *la Mera Mera Muerte* (the Big Boss Death) for a very good reason!

Your altar space could be in a guest room, bedroom, living room, attic, basement, shed in your yard, or other private nook, but it must be a space where you will not be disturbed, which can be made sacred and which can be made private and hidden from others as needed. For those who require privacy, you may follow what devotees in Mexico who were afraid of being found out have told me that they do: some created an altar in their bedroom that could have a cloth thrown over it if needed. Some had hidden altars on a tray they kept stowed under their bed, or even altars they could bolt up. This could be a shelf or drawer in a cupboard that can be kept under lock and key, or a space hidden behind a curtain or in a lockable storage cupboard.

Most Holy Death understands the need for secrecy and working in the shadows, so if you wish to remain a secret devotee, she will understand. One of her names is *Señora de las Sombras* (Lady of the Shadows), so dark and umbrous places are hers. I have kept my skeletons in my closet. At one time in my life, I had to keep my altar with numerous effigies of Most Holy Death hidden in a closet in my house because frequently others whom I knew would judge me entered. But when I opened the closet, Santa Muerte continued to smile at me from the shadows, and when I lit her votives at night, she danced her dance of death atop the shelf, grinning at me in the flickering candlelight, and I knew she did not mind.

Crucially, recall that wherever you establish your shrine, you will need to work with candles. This means fire risks will be present, so you must have an area where it is safe to light candles without setting your house or room on fire. There needs to be good ventilation so that the smoke of candles, tobacco, and incense can circulate and not overwhelm. If your statues are on a shelf, make sure the flames can flicker high and wide, without setting fire to anything.

If you are able to paint the area, this would be ideal, although it is understood that this is not always possible. Some devotees paint the ceiling with the night sky or planets in alignment with the understanding that Santa Muerte is associated with the darkness of the night, the magic of the moon, and the power of the planets. Others paint the ceiling purple, as this is the color of spirituality, and the walls black, as this is the color of protection and will ensure your sacred space is safeguarded. This is not essential.

Mexican altar to Santa Muerte featuring the typical offerings, such as apples, flowers, and tequila.

In terms of the space required, in Mexico, most shamans have a dedicated building or chapel where they worship la Santa, but most devotees do not. Devotees have small altars, or if they are more affluent, a large one. What you decide to have is dependent on you and your budget, but when first establishing it, give yourself enough space to expand with time as your relationship with her deepens and you add to your collection of

Santa Muerte paraphernalia. Having said that, a large and sumptuous altar is not necessary.

In Mexico, the majority of devotees I have met lived most modestly on small salaries. I learned one of the greatest lessons of all about Santa Muerte that I impart to you here. With *la Niña* (the Girl) as she is often called, it is not the quantity of material offerings that count, nor the number of elaborate or expensive statues, fancy candles, or other embellishments that adorn her altar that are important. It is literally the thought that counts: the fervor of your faith, your devotion, and prayer.

What matters to Santa Muerte most is dedication and spiritual commitment, namely your devotion to Death. She judges nobody. This is not a faith where she would ever hold a lack of riches or shortage of expensive items on her altar against you. This is why the simplest of offerings are acceptable but also the most important. For example, as will be explained, water is a key offering to la Santa. *El agua es vida* is what the *curandera* with the riverside shrine told me—"water is life." As such, water should be regularly refreshed—it costs next to nothing—but gifting her this vital element with care is of utmost importance. Daily refreshment allows energies to flow through your shrine. Small gestures are noticed by la Santa. Sharing a meal, a cup of coffee, a cigarette, a joint, or an alcoholic libation with her—placing them on her altar or even sitting by her as you both enjoy these delights—is always appreciated. These quotidian acts are a way of bonding with her.

Saint Death is not a folk saint who can be worked with inconsistently, so for results, although modest offerings are important (and you may choose to spoil her with a lavish bouquet of flowers should she come through for you), what is more crucial is that you commit to her, build a relationship. One lifelong devotee I met had a modest altar to Santa Muerte. Nevertheless, his dedication and connection to her were so deep that when he lit a cigarette for her, before her statuette, we both saw the image of Most Holy Death appear in the wafting smoke, smiling, her mantle swaying around her. He told me, "Prayer and faith is at the foundation of it all." Indeed, a month of nightly committed prayer to la Santa Muerte with a plain, cheap, white candle lit in her honor is worth more than an expensive bottle of tequila, a dozen roses, and no prayers. With dedication to her, you will reap, with the aid of her scythe, great rewards, riches, and miracles. She will give you as much as you give her. Therefore, consider this before you set up your altar, and ensure it is a space where such deep devotion to Death can take place.

As much as possible, use materials that are of natural origin when you set up your shrine and avoid manmade, artificial materials. For example, choose a wooden table, not a plastic one, and a cotton cloth as a table cover, not a synthetic one. Place your water in a glass receptable and select a silver, wooden, clay, or metal incense burner. There are various reasons for such choices, both practical and spiritual. To begin with, synthetic materials are far more flammable, and burning candles around such materials is not safe. But above all, natural materials, such as cotton or wood, attract earth energies, forces that are positive and powerful and will aid in your spells and prayers.

The *curandera* who lives on Atoyac River had chosen a place of nature for her shrine because, as she detailed, Most Holy Death connects with the elements. The folk saint needs to have items representing the four elements on her altar: water (you will give an offering of water; you may also place seashells if you wish to link to the sea), fire (the flames of candles), air/wind (incense, cigarettes, and cigars), and earth (fruits, stones, clay items, and wooden figures). She advised me that wooden statues and those made of stone, such as obsidian, are among the most powerful, because although Saint Death is celestial, she also is deeply chthonic. Many statues made from these materials are available; in Mexico, they are also available in resin, which is a good material, but plastic is not. Therefore, make sure you avoid synthetic items such as those made of plastic.

The minimum, basic item required to establish your altar is a flat space upon which you can set up your altar. As mentioned, this needs to be some place where you can safely light candles. In Mexico, many devotees use a wooden table, often adorned with a tablecloth that falls to the floor. Of note is that the cloth must, ideally, reach the bottom of the legs of the table and not halfway. In Mexico, these cloths are usually made of cotton, but if you cannot afford one, or do not have time to obtain it at first, a bare wooden table is acceptable, and you may choose to paint it.

Alcove altar to Santa Muerte: simple but effective

Some devotees use a shelf or an alcove that provides ample space and height to burn votives without causing risks. The space needs to be large enough to contain at least one image or statue of *la Madrina*, as well as some of the items described below. This is the space where you will honor Santa Muerte, so it should not be so tucked away that you cannot visit it daily. It is not a space that you want to forget. As stated, Holy Death does not like to be ignored. You must be willing to stop by and speak to her daily, as well as pray to her frequently, for her to take care of your petitions and miracles. A friendly "hello" in the morning when you first see her and a "goodnight" before you go to bed, as you would wish any loved one in your house, and ideally a prayer, are always welcomed and should be part of your day.

Offerings are vital to Santa Muerte and are a way of pleasing and communicating as well as working with her. The next section details the kinds of offerings that are given in Mexico, such as candy, apples, alcohol, and flowers. While you should always give general offerings when you are praying for something specific and working magic with specific candles and Santa Muerte statues, you may choose to align your oblations more specifically with your goals and needs. A guide as to how to do this is outlined in chapters four and five.

Essential Items for Starting an Altar

* A statue of Santa Muerte and/or an image; you may also have a prayer card (see chapter five on colors and poses to choose before purchasing). She should be placed in the center of the table or shelf.

* Paintings and drawings are a bonus. Devotees in Mexico often adorn their altars with statues and artwork related to Saint Death. If you have a printer or know someone who does or have obtained a printed image of her, you may even start with just this, until you have time and money to invest and choose the right statue(s). You may draw or paint one if you are so inspired as an artist. The statue or image should be the focal point of your intentions, prayers, and attentions.

* A table (ideally made of wood), shelf, or alcove.

* A cloth (ideally of cotton or other natural material). Good options are red, purple, or black (optional for shelves and alcoves but recommended for tables)

* Incense. Copal is recommended; you can also use palo santo sticks. You can buy Santa Muerte incense sticks from botanicas or online. See the *hierbateria* (plant pharmacy) later for specific plants to burn for your spiritual needs.

* An incense holder or other bowl or pot where you can burn herbal offerings.

* Matches or a lighter. Please never light your candles directly with a lighter; only matches or lit incense sticks are allowed.

* Candle(s). Again, please consult chapter five on colors to choose candles.

* A large drinking glass or a vase made of glass that is always filled with fresh water.

* Offerings of foods. You may choose between the following: bread, buns, sweet loaves, cakes, fruit (especially apples and sweet fruits), corn, nuts, candy, and chocolate. Soda is also favored by la Santa, as she has a sweet tooth.

* Offerings of flowers. A bouquet of roses is always appreciated.

* A glass or bottle of alcohol, especially tequila, mezcal, Mexican beer (bottles must be left open), or other hard liquor.

* Tobacco, cigarettes, or cigars. She also likes joints, and you can light them and let her smoke by placing them in her hand, mouth, or other suitable place. You may also practice what is known as *sahumacion* (fumigation), where you blow the smoke of a *puro* (cigar), a cigarette, or joint over her and her images; this purifies them. If you do not like smoke in your house, this offering is not vital, and you may offer her incense smoke instead, or you may choose to place Santa Muerte in an outdoor setting and let her smoke by placing the tobacco/joint in her hand and letting her puff.

* Cash. This is not always present on all altars, but some devotees like to place money as an offering to draw riches, especially bank notes. Santa Muerte likes US dollars. Although notes are ideal, small change will also be accepted. Notes can be pinned onto your effigy's gown if you wish.

Optional

* A separate effigy of an owl to be placed at la Santa's feet to serve her personally and allow you to have additional wisdom, clarity, and vision through her.

* Shells, stones, gems, crystals, or other natural decorative items that have a special link to the earth or sea.

* A photo of yourself or others whom you may be working on with Santa Muerte. This photo must not dwarf the saint or be placed above la Santa Muerte. Her superior status must be recognized spatially.

* A photo or item belonging to a deceased loved one whom you were and remain deeply connected to, as you may speak to them through the skeleton saint and also call on them to guide you.

* A box (wooden, metal, or other natural material). Although not all devotees use a box, this is recommended, as it is multipurpose. First, you can stand your Santa Muerte statue on it, allowing her to be elevated like a queen among the other items on the altar. Second, it can be useful to store items that clutter her space such as matches, incense packets, and other objects. You may also write prayers and place them in the box if you wish to conceal them from prying eyes. You can "turbo charge" your altar by placing powerful items in it, such as graveyard dirt.

   You can also energize this box with bones, earth, and stones from a graveyard, archaeological ruin, or other sacred site; or other items like gem stones. Bones are useful for healing bone ailments and for working *brujeria*. Some devotees place items belonging to a naturally deceased loved one on their altar or in this box, such as the ashes of the dearly departed in a jar or vial; you may call on these loved ones to help you and connect with you through Santa Muerte. Not all devotees do this in Mexico, and this is usually reserved for those who wish to work *hechizos* (spells).

* Skull icons, known as *calaveras*. These should be made of natural materials—for example, ceramic clay, *barro negro* (black clay), or wood.

* A cross.

* A Santa Muerte rosary.

* A horseshoe. I have occasionally seen some devotees put horseshoes on their altars for luck.

* A mirror. It may be used to see more clearly and deflect evil energy.

Optional *Hierbateria* (Herbal Items)

Curanderismo (folk healing) is an important part of traditional Santa Muerte practice, especially in rural and Indigenous Mexico. Many devotees and *curanderos* use herbs, oils, and bulbs for protection and healing. They correspond with what you feel you most need, so choose your offering in line with this. Preparing herbs, whether for burning as incense or for cleansing your altar, is working a spell in and of itself, and will add potency to your work. You may burn the dried leaves of plants listed here as incense in accordance with the prayers you select and needs you have, but you may also place the items suggested immediately below on Santa Muerte's altar.

Offerings given to Santa Muerte and placed on her altar for her:

* Glasses of olive oil (for health)

* Garlic bulbs (for protection)

* Open pots or vials containing honey (for sweetness)

* Fresh basil leaves. These should be on their stalk (for cleansing). You may place them on the altar, but you can also use them, wafting them over statues and around your body in ritual for cleansing.

* Sticks of cinnamon (for love and sex)

* Aloe vera leaves (for cleansing negative energy and good luck in your house and business)

Herbs to Burn as Incense for Specific Purposes
or Use in Herbal Water or Herbal Baths

You may choose to burn dried herbs as incense for your particular requirements (see the next chapter); here is a list of basics:

* Cedar: to bless the house or any new space you are working in

* Copal: to provide purification and protection

* Garlic peel: to rid envy and associated bad energy

* Juniper: to energize and reinvigorate body and mind

* Laurel: for abundance and prosperity

* Mint: to clear an anxious mind

* Mugwort: to encourage lucid dreams and to connect with la Santa in the dreamworld

* Rose petals: to bring love, passion, and sexual desire

* Rosemary and lavender: to cleanse the space of viruses, bacteria, and illness

* Rue: to rid the space of bad energy

* Sage: to transmute and cleanse energy

* Sweet palm: to bring sweetness and harmony

Prior to conducting any important ritual, you must cleanse yourself and your altar with incense by wafting it all over yourself, from top to toe, and also diffusing the plumes of smoke over your ritual space and statue(s). Please note these herbs are often used in cleansing baths by devotees I met in Mexico. I will elaborate on this in more detail in the cleansing rituals section on page 41.

Some devotees, as mentioned, share their food with Santa Muerte. In Mexico, I have seen devotees leave plates of food and cups of coffee for Santa Muerte, sharing their breakfasts, lunches, and dinners. The dishes they leave are typical Mexican ones, often accompanied by rice or tortillas, depending on the dish. Foods include tamales (a dish made of seasoned meat contained in a cornmeal dough pocket and steamed or baked in corn husks or banana leaves) or quesadilla (a cheese-filled tortilla that is heated until the cheese melts). People also leave regional specialties: those from Sonora and Sinaloa may leave *cahuamanta* (a skate stew), while people from Veracruz leave *chilpachole* (a thick seafood soup), and people from Oaxaca leave *mole* (a sort of saucy stew concocted with many spices and herbs). Some devotees outside of Mexico buy or attempt to make Mexican delicacies, in order to honor Santa Muerte's heritage. Whether you choose to do so or to leave other dishes is up to you. Either way, you should assess if they are well received. If bad events happen soon after gifting a dish, you will know it was not liked; conversely, if luck appears to favor you thereafter, this is a sign of approval.

If you are a smoker, you should not smoke alone at home; you must always consider sharing a cigarette, cigar, or joint with her. You may also leave marijuana buds on her altar, whether it is by her side or on her statue. She will appreciate it. Do not leave any overly sour items on the altar, such as lemon, unless required for a spell. Remember that the altar is a living space representing your relationship with the world and Santa Muerte. If you leave sour items on it, then sour things will come to you. If you leave salt, your life will become salted. The only time salt is acceptable is with a shot glass of tequila accompanied by lime or during the Day of the Dead. If you let things rot on your shrine, things in your life will putrefy.

Getting the Altar Ready

When getting the altar ready, make sure it is at a quiet time. Some devotees recommend early Tuesday morning. Others prefer the night, particularly on the first day of a new moon, to ensure positive energy is suffused into the altar. But above all, this must be a tranquil moment when no one will disturb you. Turn off your phone, turn off the TV, switch off the computer. If you live with others, advise them not to disturb you. You may wish to put on music. You might find songs dedicated to Santa Muerte online. There are many *narcocorridos* (a type of ballad) which honor la Santa Muerte that she enjoys. "La Santísima Muerte" by Beto Quintanilla is a classic example.

You may find rap songs honoring her, such as by artists like Nano. There is also pre-Hispanic music and other esoteric music. I recommend only such spiritual music and advise against music that does not match her energy, like Irish jigs! Over time you will learn what music Santa Muerte responds to. Let me share an anecdote to illustrate this. One day, while cleaning my home, I decided to put on some African Soukous music. When I began tidying the room where her altar is, I moved the portable speaker to a shelf just opposite Santa Muerte's space. Suddenly, the speaker started crackling, and the music kept cutting out. It sounded horrendous. As soon as I changed the music to Jorge Reyes's *Rituales Prehispanicos,* all the ruckus stopped, and the melodies filled the air. Santa Muerte made herself clear: she wanted sacred music of Mexican origins in her space, not Soukous.

To ready your room for Santa Muerte, first, make sure the area is cleansed physically: dust the room, clean and mop the floor. You do not want to invite the great power of Death herself into a dirty space. You would not welcome a new houseguest into a place of squalor, so make sure everything is clean, including the table or shelf where you will set up your altar. Second, cleanse the space spiritually, purifying with incense, especially copal and other such incense. You may also add the smoke of a cigar. Imagine, as you sweep incense over the space, the area being purified with her scythe and all negative energy being cut away. Also imagine her long cloak protecting you and the space, rendering it sacred. You should also begin to address Santa Muerte at this time through her statue, image, or in general, telling her you are preparing this space for her and informing her you are dedicating yourself to her and asking for her permission to do so. Pay attention to any noises, things falling, or other signs from her.

Then ready your table or shelf. Clean this with herbal water (see the section "Ritual Cleansing of Your Altar"), ammonia, or colognes such as *siete machos* or *agua de Florida* (Florida water). In Mexico, the latter are considered not just cleansers or perfumes but also capable of ridding negative energy, so they should be used regularly to cleanse the space. After this, if using a table, cover it in cloth. Run incense through and around the cloth before placing it on the table without getting ash on it or burning it!

If you wish to use a box, then place it in the middle of the table. You may choose to cover it with more colored cloth so that it is hidden from prying eyes. On top of this box, place your statue of Santa Muerte. You might want to use a box with a lock and key if you need to store secret spell items and prayers safely away from snoopers. This box is the heart of your shrine and can be used to keep sacred objects.

Around and below Santa Muerte, place the other items recommended. Use candles and flowers according to the color scheme required (see chapter five on choosing these items; a white candle is highly recommended when beginning). You should also give her a glass or vase of fresh water; as Santa Muerte is a skeleton, she is perpetually thirsty and her water must be kept clean. Dirty water is a sign of negative energy and must be discarded. Water that turns a nasty color warns of danger. Water with air bubbles signifies she is pleased, or that contented spirits are present. Water should always be plentiful as it absorbs energy and allows that energy to flow through your altar; it must be discarded and replenished to refresh the energy.

Keep an eye on offerings daily, observing whether they are appreciated. You must learn to watch the items on your altar, as it is through them that she communicates with you:

* If her statue moves, she is giving you a sign she is present.

* Flowers that immediately wither are a sign that she does not like them; on the other hand, flowers that stay fresh for an unusual amount of time are blooms she likes.

* Items that fall off the table, or posters affixed to the walls nearby that drop down, are also unwanted or herald a warning.

This space is a place of communication between you and la Santa. You must give to her and honor her in this space, and she will speak to you through such signs and through the candles.

No book can detail all the ways in which Santa Muerte may speak to you, so you must learn to visit the altar often and observe it for signs from her. One shaman noted how images appeared on her shrine in offerings. For example, one morning a brown patch in the shape of Saint Death appeared on an apple she had gifted her the night before, and she knew la Santa had blessed her prayer. Another day, cigarette ash fell from the saint's hand into a pattern that looked like an owl's face with preternaturally large eyes. She knew la Santa was warning her to keep her eyes peeled for any negative situation around her. She was rewarded when someone tried to steal from her and she caught them by keeping a close eye about.

Another devotee detailed how particular kinds of roses lasted very long on her altar; this, he explained, was because la Santa loved them most of all. Dreams of the Powerful Lady directly after a ritual to Santa Muerte are her means of sending you a message, the content of which will reveal the ritual's success or not. You should also pay attention to the smoke of tobacco and incense because her face or other symbols may appear in the plumes. Animal omens may also be a sign of la Niña—in particular, owls, which may hoot or fly by your window. These are a sign she is watching over you. You must discover and be open to the ways she will reach out to you.

If you find insects in the water or libations, please consult the "Insect and Animal Omens" section, beginning on page 93, as these are omens. For example, once when I was at a shrine, an offering of beer I gifted to la Santa was found inundated with ants the next day. The owner of the shrine told me that this signified envy, which made sense because someone was spreading malicious gossip about me at the time. I was advised to cleanse myself with a cleansing bath of a rue infusion, the incense of copal, as well as to light candles and recite prayers to combat envy. This anecdote illustrates the importance of taking note of signs and acting on them to ensure any bad energy is detracted and dealt with.

Also, place a glass of alcohol, such as tequila or mezcal, or beer, on the altar. In Mexico, I have also seen bourbon, rum, and sugar cane-derived drinks such as Huasteco on altars. Other hard liquors such as whiskey are also acceptable, as is beer; Corona is one brand I have often seen in shrines. These libations must be refreshed regularly, and should be offered as thanks when she comes through for you. Watch as they disappear, signifying she is imbibing them. If the glasses or bottles mysteriously fall over or the libations never evaporate, these are signs that she did not like that brand and that you should offer a different one. When you have a drink, whether it is beer or hard liquor, always consider sharing with Santa Muerte. Although she is dead, Santa Muerte wants you to enjoy life, and she enjoys enjoying life with you. She is not judgmental, and if you are partying or having a wild Saturday night, she wants to be part of that party! Drink with her, smoke with her, and dance at her side. She will not chastise you for it; instead, you may notice an extra twinkle in her hollow eye or a cheeky grin!

Place some foods on your altar—apples, sweet fruits, corn, buns, honey, candy, and chocolate are all welcome. Do not let these items perish, and do not place already-rotting fruit on your altar. Old food will not be tolerated. Likewise, wilting flowers must be discarded. When you remove old offerings such as chocolates and other foods, do not throw them away. If possible, donate to the needy or give them to foodbanks. I have had children ask me for them too, and with Santa Muerte's express approval, this is allowed. No longer wanted dishes of food can also be fed to stray cats and dogs. Food should not be grabbed off the altar to eat, unless in a pinch. A devotee once told me she had gifted a bottle of water to Santa Muerte. When her water was cut off, that was all she had left to drink and *la Madrina* let her drink it. Offerings must be changed at least once a month.

Occasionally, I have heard of devotees in Mexico who left a special rose on her altar that was gifted to them by a loved one, and they let it dry out and remain on the altar. But this is risky for a neophyte, and it is ill advised to do so unless you have established a deep relationship with her. I kept dried roses a loved one offered me on my shrine for a long time, as they reminded me of that bond, but as much as I adored them, one day I decided to discard them along with all other old offerings, replacing them with fresh roses. That day, my path suddenly opened, and a miracle was granted to me. I learned that old offerings mean old energy and that they can cause stagnation. Fresh gifts mean new energy that Most Holy Death will convert into blessings for you.

After offering the food and beautiful flowers, you may now place any additional items listed. An owl effigy, a photo of yourself and/or your loved one, and indeed this book may be kept on the shrine or in the box below Santa Muerte for safe keeping. No other books or papers should be kept on the shrine unless they are mystical and directly related to Holy Death, or to a petition you seek her help with, such as a written prayer or a court summons. Once you have set up your altar, if you tolerate smoke, you may place a cigarette or joint on your Santa Muerte statue, resting it in her hand, or on the globe or other appropriate area, and allow her to puff on it. Alternatively, you may choose to blow cigar smoke over the altar to purify it.

The final stage of establishing the shrine is to say a prayer to the skeleton saint and to light a candle. The white candle is the most recommended, but a *siete potencias*, the seven-colored Santa Muerte candle, is also an excellent choice. A general prayer is a good choice, and you may perform a novena, a nine-day prayer, which is recited every day for nine days, to win her good graces immediately. Either way, when you first establish this altar, it is recommended that, as in Mexico, you visit it every day and honor Santa Muerte for at least nine consecutive days. This you must do before starting any spell work with her.

Blood Pact Ritual

A secret practice that a witch deeply devoted to death taught me is the blood pact ritual. This witch lived high in the mountains, in the Sierra Madre del Sur, and it was said by the people in the village that she had never been a young girl and had been ancient as long as anyone in the community had known her. No one could verify her actual age. But I was told that, regardless of her advanced years, she never changed, looking the same despite the advance of time. She exuded a power I have never felt before. Her long silver hair trailed down beyond her waist, and her gaunt face wore a determined expression. Despite her many years upon this planet, she had fierce eyes, a spry gait, and more vigor in her than many of the local youth. Many feared her, for it was known that she could look into the seeds of time and see which would grow and which would not. Her hexes were said to be deadly to anyone who crossed her. Such was her love for Santa Muerte, she told me, that she had dedicated herself to her worship many decades ago. After I had known her for numerous years, she told me it was time I learn to connect with Santa Muerte at the most profound level possible.

In Mexico, the birthplace of Santa Muerte, only the most advanced *curanderos* and witches who have dedicated their lives to death have heard of it, and even some of those who know of it do not dare perform the ritual. This is a deeply occult and clandestine way to finalize the creation of your altar and your connection with Santa Muerte. This witch shared this ritual with me, as she said I was ready to deepen my bond with Death. I had proved myself, and she invited me to share it with those who also feel ready, but to warn them of the consequences of its power.

I definitely do not recommend this ritual to the neophyte, nor the amateur honing their skills, and absolutely discourage the person who likes to work with multiple spirits, saints, or deities from conducting this ceremony. To repeat: it is not for the faint of heart, nor for those who are polytheistic, as this blood pact is an act of complete loyalty to Holy Death, a promise to be devoted exclusively to her till your death and complete union with her. This pact forges forever a deep bond between you and Santa Muerte that no other deity or person may interfere with, compete with, nor replace. I do not advise this pact to those who are new to Santa Muerte. Most people are liable to change their mind about their spiritual practices over the course of their lifetime; hence, this pact is not for most people. Indeed, the ritual is rarely referred to unless you become deeply initiated into the mysteries of Santa Muerte. I therefore repeat, as I cannot emphasize this enough, the ritual is only for the most committed, lifelong devotee who is sure they will only worship Holy Death, exclusively, and no other deity, until the day they die. If you decide to do this pact, you must keep this secret till your grave and speak of your pact with only the most trusted fellow devotees, if at all.

This blood pact with Death must be done on a full moon at midnight, after you have fully cleansed and purified yourself. The time must be quiet, the energy must be deep, and you must be in fresh, clean clothes. You must enter into a deep trance-like state beforehand and make many offerings of a lavish kind from numerous bouquets of flowers to foods, fruits, and libations of all kinds; you must cover the altar with these opulent offerings and include both essential and optional items. You must light many candles of all colors, including a red, a black, and a white one, but ideally all colors should be present. The red should be at the center of the altar. You must pray reverently and repeatedly to Most Holy Death, honor her by name as queen, creator, and power supreme. You must then gift her your blood.

You may choose to slash your palm with a knife or other blade, or prick your finger deeply with a needle so as to have several large and generous droplets of blood, and then offer her the sanguine fluid by letting the blood drip into a vial or other vessel. A small globule will not suffice. Women may choose to offer their menstrual blood in a chalice or other vessel for that purpose but ideally should add this to blood from a slashed hand or pricked finger. This mixture will be extremely potent. It is advised that menstrual blood be from the first few days of your bleeding when your blood is at its thickest, bright and fresh. You must tell Santa Muerte humbly that this blood offering is to create a deep, lifelong pact with her and only her. If you wish, you may also honor her by giving your main statue a name at this point that you will address her with from thereon out. You must acknowledge all her powers and state that you will serve her, and only her, forever, until she takes you in her final embrace of Death.

Such an offering and ritual must be opened and completed with a prayer dedicated to her, not one where you ask for anything but simply a prayer of thanks (such as in the prayers in this book; see chapter six on page 130). The blood pact is a deep commitment, and you must be aware that if you do this, you will be attached to and in service of Santa Muerte your entire life and cannot turn to other deities of any kind, apart from God, with whom la Santa works and to whom you must always show respect. If you do veer from the path of Death or start praying to other entities, she will punish you for your betrayal in the most severe fashion, bringing you bad luck for the rest of your life. For this reason, I reiterate, this blood pact is not recommended unless you are deadly serious.

The ritual can be carried out at a later date, after many months or preferably years when you are sure you are ready to dedicate your life to death. The reason this is such a serious commitment is that it is not a promise that can be simply severed, forgotten, or abandoned should you change your mind, meet a partner who does not approve of your devotion, or forget or move on from the folk saint of death due to other such life events. You cannot simply start working with other deities. Although I have included an unbonding ritual to "break up" with Most Holy Death in chapter eight of this book, as it is recognized that sometimes we move on spiritually and not all can bond with Mother Death, this ritual does not work if you have blood-pacted with her.

Setting Up an Altar to Santa Muerte, Working with It and Cleansing It

Saint Death will punish you if you make a blood pact to her and do not make good on this commitment and overlook her in the future. This could mean things go wrong for you; you might lose your job, your house, your spouse; sustain a severe injury; or suffer other such tragedies. A blood pact is the ultimate, unbreakable making of a bond with Death herself, and you will have to serve her with deep devotion and dedication until you die and join her for eternity. For this reason, I really do not recommend the blood pact to anyone, unless you are ready for a serious, lifelong commitment. For the neophyte, simply starting out, naming your statues, keeping a clean altar, and being generous and regular in your offerings are sufficient to bond with Santa Muerte such that she listens to your prayers and helps you in spell work.

I want to add an anecdote to make clear why this blood pact must be taken seriously. I was told it by a *curandera*. A woman frequently came to her to ask her to work magic with Santa Muerte. The woman, whom we'll call M, had been devoted to death for fifteen years. The *curandera* saw that she was very serious in her worship. M asked the *curandera* how to bond more deeply with Santa Muerte, given her business was in serious jeopardy, for she risked going bankrupt. The *curandera* told M about the blood pact with Holy Death, which would deepen her bond and ritual work with Santa Muerte. M did this and vowed to worship only the Pretty Girl for the rest of her days. Soon after, a miracle happened: M's business suddenly flourished with many customers coming to her doors and suppliers granting her extremely favorable prices. M's business expanded in the year that followed, and she eventually moved to larger premises. Everything in her life was going perfectly; she had a wonderful husband, two healthy children, and a large house.

M, however, began to stray from Santa Muerte. She became interested in the orisha Yemanja and—having difficulty conceiving a third child—decided to create a small altar for this Goddess of the Sea, whose specialties include fertility. Nine months later, M. had a baby girl and was delighted. But Santa Muerte was not. Two months after the baby was born, M took a trip north to visit her family, traveling alone with only the newborn to see her mother. The trip passed without incident, but she could not reach her family on the phone while away. She was worried. Upon arriving home, she was horrified to see that it had burned to ashes. Her husband and two other children had died in the blaze. She lost everything.

Ritual Cleansing of Your Altar

Your Santa Muerte altar must be maintained and kept clean if spells are to work and prayers are to be heard. You must also do personal cleansing work, as your own energy should be kept clean. Do not cleanse your altar if you feel you have attracted negative energy to yourself without first doing a ritual of personal cleansing. Your altar, and your statues (as described in chapter four), should be cleansed at least once a month, ideally on a full moon or a new moon, but if you feel much negativity around you, you may choose to do so on another date. If you can on this same day, you should cleanse your statues, as detailed in the "Moon-bathing Ritual" section, wherein it is explained how to purify the effigies using the power of the moon.

The reason an altar must be cleansed spiritually is that it attracts energy, therefore, negative vibes can cling to it as can the energy of spells you have worked there. When you are praying or undertaking new spell work, such a backlog of energy can prevent those spells from succeeding. Also, as detailed in the introduction, Most Holy Death likes to be bathed and kept fresh, as well as having her altar, which you can think of as her house, kept tidy.

To clean your altar, remove every single item from it. Discard offerings. If you have a tablecloth atop your altar, this too may be removed and laundered. After all is removed, wipe down the space with a soapy cloth and clean the floor as well as the surrounding area, if possible, of all dust and incense ash and so on.

Following this, use the herbal waters detailed in the "Ritual to Awaken Your Statues and Cleansing Ritual" section, such as the elixir of rosemary, rue, and basil or other herbal combinations, or *siete machos*, ammonia, or *agua de Florida* (Florida water), which can be bought in most botanicas or online to spiritually cleanse the area. It is best to soak a cloth in one of these liquids to wipe down the table, alcove, or shelf. I have heard of devotees who use Holy Water outside of Mexico, but this is almost unheard of in Mexico, even if it is used occasionally in spell work where total spiritual cleaning is required. All these liquids are used for cleansing and remove bad vibes; they also protect the area from negative energy. You should also use this soaked cloth to dust down any effigies or ornaments. As you do so, cleanse them spiritually of all evil energies.

Following this, place all the items back on your altar. Ensure you have emptied all vases and glasses of water and replaced the water with a fresh supply. It is recommended that you have a good amount of water on your shrine as this collects energy and can help you with the flow of energy, recycling this through the altar, and then allowing you to discard negative energy. Take note of the color of the water as you discard it or watch for the presence of insects. If you notice bad omens, it is important to cleanse yourself, not only your altar, and ask Santa Muerte to protect you from this bad energy. As mentioned, you must pay attention to water. If there are bubbles in your water, that means Holy Death is happy with you and you have pleased her.

Make sure, once everything is back on the altar, that some fresh offerings are placed on the shrine at this time. They need not be extravagant. If you can only afford a few candies, that is fine, although flowers are always welcome. After this, it is also vital that you cleanse the altar using smoke. Incense and tobacco should be used to cleanse the altar at this time. For those averse to tobacco, incense can be used. Pass the incense smoke all over your altar and then suffuse each ornament with the plumes of incense smoke, bathing your Santa Muerte statue(s) to fully purify them.

If you are open to working with tobacco, you may now blow smoke over your statue(s). You can use a cigar, cigarette, or even a joint containing marijuana. You may also choose to give your statue(s) a cigarette, cigar, or spliff to puff on. Place it in her hand or lodge it in the crook of her elbow. In Mexico, I have seen witches and *curanderos* place cigarettes in the mouths and even ears of larger statues. If your statue allows for this, you can do so. Note whether your statue enjoys the cigarette—that is, whether she finishes it because it is appreciated or whether it just goes out because she does not like it. There may be brands of tobacco she prefers, and it is a good sign if she finishes her smoke.

At this time, you may also choose to light a white Santa Muerte candle, which is cleansing, or you can use an aloe vera candle or seven-herb candle (*veladora 7 hierbas*). In Mexico, aloe vera (known as *sabila*) is used traditionally by *curanderos* in rituals of cleansing. You can use it not only to cleanse the space but may also use it to cleanse and purify your body of bad vibes, as described in chapter four. As stated earlier, fresh basil can also be wafted around to remove energy and then placed on the altar. At this time, if you feel you have been under spiritual attack or afflicted by negative energy, it is a good time to say a protective prayer to Most Holy Death. This is also an ideal time to begin a novena or work a new spell. As your altar is cleansed, it is receptive to new energy, and the Powerful Lady is happy to begin bonding with you and work with you on your goals. See the next few chapters for prayers, spells, and rituals that will help you achieve your desires through devotion to death.

CHAPTER FOUR

Working with Santa Muerte

In this chapter, you will learn about what statues to purchase, rituals to awaken your statues, how to name them, times of the day or night to work with la Santa, and how to understand her key attributes.

Purchasing

Although you may commence your devotion with a printed image of Santa Muerte at the center of your altar, eventually you should begin working with a statue. Buying your first statue may seem a little daunting, but this section will make the most important considerations clear. Purchasing the most extravagant, expensive, or flashy statue should not be your goal. Instead, you should pay attention to the way you feel about buying the statue and its mystical provenance, trusting your spiritual intuition rather than your wallet. Money should not be a concern as, for Santa Muerte, the most powerful statue is not the largest or most expensive one. It is the statue that is of good provenance but most of all, the statue into which you invite the spirit of Most Holy Death to enter by focusing your energy on it and giving her offerings, reciting prayers, performing rituals to her, and even naming her. I cannot emphasize enough that the most vital aspect of working with a statue is to make Santa Muerte's spirit feel that she is so thoroughly welcomed and adored that she chooses to suffuse it. To do this, you must build a loving relationship with her through the effigy, meditate upon her skeletal form, and pray to her regularly with deep devotion. Your intent, focus, attention to her, energy, love for her, respect, prayers, gifts, and gestures are some of the many ways in which Santa Muerte will determine whether she wishes to come into your statue or not. She is the Queen of Death; thus, only royal treatment is befitting.

Some devotees choose to buy statues from *curanderos* or *brujos* and request that they bless and awaken the statues for them. If you know of such spiritual specialists personally, then this is an excellent move, but if you have not met them or are unsure whether they are genuine or truly gifted in the mystical arts of Santísima Muerte, it is best to awaken the statue yourself rather than pay what is often a hefty fee to a stranger whose real intentions and powers are not known to you and who could use spell work to steal energy from you through the statue. I have watched closely and been informed of the best ways to awaken and cleanse statues, and thus recommend that you do this yourself before entrusting a cherished statue to be blessed by someone you do not know.

Of course, in Mexico the most powerful statue is not the most costly but is the one gifted by a beloved friend, family member, spouse, or lover. And not because you coerced them into giving you access to their *Amazon.com* account so you could order one with their credit card or told them to buy you that one in the botanica you saw "or it's over!" Rather, it should be that they specially selected the effigy as a gift to you, from their heart and soul to yours, wishing to protect, love, and aid you on your spiritual journey.

My first statue was gifted to me by a mystical Santa Muerte seer; it is permeated with more potency than any other statue I own. It was gifted to me the night I had a near-death experience when I crashed my car by a Santa Muerte shrine on a full moon and survived miraculously with zero injuries thanks to the power of Most Holy Death. As I walked away from the wreck into the shrine to Santa Muerte, a witch appeared from the shadows and led me in prayer to the Lady of the Shadows. We stayed deep into the night speaking of Death herself. The witch gifted me my first statue, and, soon after, I became a devotee. Though this statue is slightly faded, worn, and fairly small compared to my other statues, it is my most precious possession. On her skull, this Santa has a constant knowing grin that informs me she is watching over me and everyone else around me.

Such gifted statues of the folk saint of death are brimming with life, love, and vital energy.

I have also gifted statues to devotees I am close to and have been told they performed impressive miracles for the receiver. During the COVID-19 pandemic, I gifted a statue to a Mexican friend of mine who was having financial troubles and whose store was at risk of closing due to new regulations. Within a week of the gift, she received paperwork allowing her not only to keep her store open but also giving her financial aid.

Having said this, I suggest you be careful whom you accept statues from. I have heard of men gifting women statues just to butter them up, with ill effects. Also, a friend of mine told me of a man, Raul, dabbling in devotion, who was gifted a statue by Carmelo, who owned a market stall selling such statues in Tabasco. Carmelo co-owned his business with Nosana, a long-time supplicant of la Santa. A few months prior to Carmelo gifting the statue to Raul, Nosana and Raul fell out over a woman they both liked. When Nosana found out that Carmelo had given to Raul a statue that financially belonged half to him, he was furious. It meant a loss of income, and to add insult to injury, the statue had been gifted to Raul, who spoke ill of Nosana to all who would listen. Nosana told Santa Muerte what had happened requesting she deliver justice. The statue, rather than receiving Santa's loving spirit, was hexed. A statue received with a curse upon it can seldom be cleansed of ill intent. From that day on, Raul constantly had bad luck. From this story, you should recognize the importance of receiving gifts only from people who truly care for you and within contexts of trust.

While a gift given with unconditional love will bring much potency to your altar, one not given in this spirit will bring toxicity, curses, and bad luck to you and your family. Indeed, it is better to buy a statue than accept a poisonous gift that was given with an ulterior motive, bad intent, or some other negative energy surrounding it. On the other hand, I heard how a mother brought her daughter a red Santa Muerte because her daughter could not find a true love. After being lonely many years, within three weeks of being gifted the statue, praying to the Red Lady and giving her apples, roses, and tequila, her daughter met the love of her life and has been with him now these past twenty years in marital bliss.

All this is to say that gifts of statues are powerful. If a close friend or family member is a devotee of *la Madrina*, you may consider buying them a statue, as for a follower of the folk saint, there is no greater gift. You may with time hope that a loved one considers buying you a figurine, but as a neophyte, you cannot always expect to be regaled with a gift of death, and this is of no concern. Indeed, most devotees in Mexico will inevitably buy a Santa Muerte statue or several during their lifetime. This is why it is important to know how to pick a good effigy, and the one you select should, of course, align with your needs and lifestyle.

Colors of Statues

When you are selecting your statue, your first consideration should be the color. You will want to choose which of Santa Muerte's many aspects you work with based on the needs you have. Here I provide a brief overview to get you started. The colors are more amply detailed in chapter five, where further information is given as to how to work with the varying aspects and colors of Santa Muerte. This is so you can match your votives to your statues.

When Santa Muerte veneration first became popular in the 1980s and 1990s, her three original colors were white, black, and red, representing her distinct powers and personae. Someone I met outside of Mexico told me that these colors originate from those used in the ancient codices, such as the Codex Borgia, to depict death deities like Mictecacihuatl, and her husband Mictlantecuhtli, who, they said, were painted only in red, black, and white. The codices are manuscripts made by Indigenous peoples using dried animal skins. However, having looked up prints of the codices at my local Mexican library and having examined the imagery, I noted that the death deities were also painted in yellow and green.

Nevertheless, these three colors are universal in virtually all religions symbolizing the key elements: white represents purity, light, and bones; red represents power, passion, and blood; and black represents death, decay, darkness, and night. Some chapel owners still choose to focus only on this trio or to dedicate their shrine to one color alone, such as the infamous shrine in Hidalgo, which is dedicated to Santa Muerte in her black form. However, devotees in Mexico tend to employ a whole panoply of colors in the modern era. Most of the shrines I regularly visit across the country, from Michoacan to Acapulco, have a wide array of colors. The gold, white, black, and red statues I have found to be the most popular choices, as well as the seven-colored statue. Many devotees also love Aztec- or Indigenous-themed statues, as these are said to channel ancient powers emanating from the death deities of atavistic eras.

Most Holy Death has expanded beyond this initial trio of red, black, and white, and in the early 2000s, she started to appear in seven main colors that correspond to her *siete potencias*, or seven powers. However, in more recent times, Santa Muerte's powers have expanded once again, going beyond these seven colors to include many hues and combinations of colors. Each hue represents an aspect of her persona and powers. You can call on *la Madrina* in any of these colors, but you must build a relationship with her in that hue. If you honor her, get to know her ways, meditate on her forces, and show your devotion, she may give you gifts and miracles from her sacred power. You should also align the color of your offerings of flowers to the favors being asked if you have specific needs. Please note that most of these colors are further detailed in the "Color of Candles" section.

Color Correspondences

As you will learn, as you turn to Santa Muerte in her different color forms, there is huge difference in the work, in the interactions, and in the results as each color represents a distinct aspect of her powers, character, and virtues. Build a bond with the Santa Muerte whose color corresponds to your needs by honoring her, praying to her, and learning to understand her mystical ways, and she will reward you.

Primary Colors

Black

Black Santa Muerte helps you when you need vengeance, hexing, protection, safety, and also protection from the coronavirus. In her black gown, Santa Muerte is known as *la Niña Negra*, or the Black Girl. She is a vengeful *cabrona* (badass) and is the darkest energy form of the Skeleton Saint to work with. She is immensely powerful and can proffer protection from harm of all sorts and hex enemies. But her power can come back to you if she is not happy with you, Karma style and, as I was told by devotees, "punch you in the face if you're lucky or take out your family if you are not." She is the most respected as well as the most feared form of Holy Death across Mexico. Those who learn to work *brujeria* with her will be rewarded. Those who try to play with her without knowing what they are doing will get a smack around the head! Black Santa Muerte likes tobacco, marijuana offerings, hard booze, and rich foods.

Red

Red Santa Muerte is the Queen of love, passion, and sex. In her red guise, Santa Muerte is known as *la Niña Roja* (the Red Girl). She is saucily beguiling and literally drop-dead hot. She helps with all affairs of the heart and libido. *La Niña Roja* does not judge, so whether you are LGBTQ+ or asking for a sexual miracle, there is no notion of strict morality in the spirituality; all petitions are welcome. As will be described, for amorous petitions, it is always good to have an intimate object belonging to the person on which you wish to cast the spell. Hair, nail clippings, a piece of clothing, or other personal items are good for love spells. For sex sorcery, undergarments that have been worn and ideally soiled during sexual activities are useful. She loves red roses, strong liquor, and red apples.

White

White Santa Muerte brings purity, consecration, health, and cleansing. In her white gown, Santa Muerte is known as *la Niña Blanca* (the White Girl).

She is the purest, most gentle, and uplifting Santa to work with and is turned to for petitions that call for care, harmony, and peacefulness. She is motherly and kind. While both love magic and the malevolent magic of *la Niña Negra* can come with consequences, the White Girl's magic is beneficent. She can also illuminate your path, allowing you to see the truth or bringing you light in times of darkness. White flowers are an ideal offering for her.

Secondary Colors

Amber

Amber Santa Muerte will aid in overcoming addiction and vices (gambling, alcoholism, drug addiction, and so forth). She will help you break any bad habits, whether it is overeating or even spending too much time on social media, or with people who are bad for you, whether in love or friendship.

Black and Red

Black and red Santa Muerte reverses malevolent magic and ill fortune, sending hexes and harm back to the sender. She is less known outside Mexico, but inside the country, *la Reversible*, as she is known, is popular. She protects you by sending back negativity to those attacking you, without fearing retribution. Instead of hexing, you are just boomeranging everything back to those harming you, and often, as I will detail in the Colors of Candles section, upon its return, that energy is even more potent and dangerous. In my opinion, Most Holy Death in her red and black cloak—which, respectively, embody both domination and protection—is one of the most powerful statues to work with if you are under assault, whether physically, energetically, or psychologically.

Blue

Blue Santa Muerte gifts you with mental focus, insight, communication, wisdom, creativity and concentration. In her azure gown, she is popular with students and those whose jobs or activities require sharp mental focus or who need to tap into la Santa's sacred, creative, and communicative energy. If you have an exam, a small, blue Santa Muerte statuette would be an excellent miracle-working mascot to have on your exam desk or in your pocket. People also turn to her to improve communication when this has broken down. Personally, Blue Santa Muerte aids me in all my artistic and literary endeavors, inspiring and supporting me. She loves blue-petaled flowers.

Bone

Bone Santa Muerte, known as *Santa Muerte de Hueso* or *natural,* eases tensions, bringing you peace, harmony, and success wherever you place her. She may also help heal bones, such as fractures. *Brujos* and *curanderos* often work with this color and with bone offerings to call forth the dead and spirits. Offerings of bones are welcomed.

Brown

Brown Santa Muerte wears a robe the color of dirt. Earthy and ancient, she rules over the chthonic realms of the dead. In her brown gown, Santa Muerte can be turned to for necromancy, and communication with the underworld. If you wish to establish a deep psychic connection with Holy Death or require spiritual concentration and telepathy, bond with her. Graveyard dirt is an excellent offering for the Lady of the Shadows in this form, especially if you seek to communicate with the dead through her.

Copper

Copper Santa Muerte helps you to purge negative energies and remove obstacles, especially financial problems. She is particularly adept at improving work spaces, helping you to remove obstacles blocking business deals.

Gold

Gold Santa Muerte is generous and opulent in her gilded gown. Turn to her for any petitions related to money, prosperity, and business success. She is known as la Niña Dorada and will help you with your finances or any area where you require abundance. She will bring good fortune to your home, business, or office. Give her golden tequila, some coins, or preferably bank notes to increase your affluence and success.

Green

Green Santa Muerte is your lawyer and advocate, aiding you to obtain justice, deal with legal matters, and handle litigious trouble. In her green form, Santa Muerte is known as *la Niña Verde* (the Green Girl) or *la Justiciera* (the Righteous Lady). She can help with all matters pertaining to justice and judgment, whether it is winning a court case (even if you were in the wrong), avoiding going to court, or dealing with other matters of judgment when you want to sway people in your favor, especially in bureaucratic or other administrative situations. She helps you deal with red tape, and will bring justice in any situation where you have been wronged, whether this is with the law or in any other context.

Pink

Pink Santa Muerte is soft, sweet, and sentimental. Bond with her when you need romance, care, and tender love. She is different from the Red Girl in that she brings forth love based on deep emotional attachment, care, and soul connection as opposed to *la Niña Roja*, who is more about passion, lust, and even amorous domination by creating sexual longing in the person you enchant. Pink roses are an ideal offering.

Purple

Purple Santa Muerte is the ultimate deathly *bruja* who rules over the supernatural realms and is the sovereign of sorcery. She is also a doctor of death, healing all sorts of diseases and ailments. Bond with her for *brujeria*, to access the mystical realms and for dreamwork. Eggplant, purple berries, and purple flowers are well received.

Silver

Silver Santa Muerte is a lunar lady of luck, abundance, and imagination. She disrupts any negative energy and helps us to unblock problems related to finances, as well as to wrap up all pending business deals or problems. She channels the energy of moon magic in all its mysticism, so connect with her to draw in lunar energy. Offer her silver items and sparkling things.

Transparent

Transparent Santa Muerte is a a diaphanous Goddess. Her ball gown, made of see-through, colorless resin with glitter within it, sparkles and glistens. Turn to her when you need to see clearly into the heart of things; this could be both in material and immaterial matters. If you need more factual information, for example, on whether to make a decision, such as buying a house or car, you can turn to *la Transparente*, as she is known. She is mystical and ethereal, aiding you with psychic work when you need to penetrate into invisible cosmic realms to know of mysteries, tune into higher mental states, or work through lucid dreaming. She will cleanse a space and keep pure energies flowing. Water is the offering par excellence for her. Transparent and sparkling stones, glass objects, and libations such as silver tequila and mezcal also enhance her powers. Moreover, her transparency makes her versatile as paired with the candle color of your choice. During prayer work and *brujeria*, she may take on any powers you wish. I have also bought lamps and lightbulbs of different colors to shine them through my transparent statue so that she becomes illuminated in those hues. The effect is iridescent and beautiful.

Yellow

Yellow Santa Muerte is the lady of success. She will help you solve problems, open doors, and bring triumph to all the areas of your life—whether in financial or other matters. She is excellent for when goals need to be achieved because she brings positive energy to all endeavors. Gift yellow flowers, foods, and candies.

Multicolored, or Seven Powers *(Siete Potencias)*

Seven-powered Santa Muerte's robe is decorated in seven different layers of color, signifying multiple interventions on all the fronts listed previously. She is truly the Powerful Lady, for she works miracles on multiple fronts simultaneously to bring synergy. She will intervene in all domains of your life to bring things together into perfect harmony so that you can have the best possible outcome. If you are unsure what figure to buy or unable to afford the multiple colors you want, *la siete potencias* is for you. After all, you can never go wrong with the Lady of the Seven Powers on your side!

······✳······

You should choose your first Santa Muerte statue according to this color code, but as just stated, the multicolor-cloaked skeleton saint, known as *siete potencias*, is an excellent choice for the unsure or thrifty neophyte as she is cost-effective and multipurpose. *La siete potencias* will allow you to receive all of Santa Muerte's powers without the need for several figurines on your altar. Devotees in Mexico relate that a statue of one single color will allow you to focus fully on Santa Muerte's particular power and bond with her more deeply in that aspect, but if you don't have the space or the money for many effigies, or when you need to align different aspects of your life so that they come into perfect harmony, then the *siete potencias* statue is the color of choice. As detailed later, if you are able to dress your effigy of *La Niña* yourself, you can also buy a statue whom you outfit in the colors you require.

Origin and Material

Your second consideration should be the provenance and material of the statue. I have found that those effigies obtained from Mexico are much more powerful. Usually made of resin, they are sold charged, whereas those made in China and elsewhere are not. I was repeatedly informed by *brujos* that it is important that you buy a statue that is charged. What does this mean? When a statue is charged, the manufacturer places what in Spanish is called *una carga* (a charge) at the base of the statue. This consists of a transparent glazed section, visible to the naked eye, that is loaded with seeds and charms.

A *curandero* clarified that the *carga* is essential to any Santa Muerte statue as the charge imbues the statue with power. The seeds, often mustard seeds and others, such as circassian seeds (*Adenanthera pavonina*, also known as red lucky seeds as they are believed to bring luck, especially in love), are from plants that grow fast and are hardy both in their seed and plant form. This charge ensures that your prayers and spells, just like these seeds, will take root fast and grow strong, blooming with celerity, like the fast-flourishing mustard flower, to give you the miracles you seek. The charms and symbols, such as little coins, a horseshoe, a crucifix, or other such items, bring good luck, protect you from bad energy, and also empower your work with the statue. Think of this *carga* as the battery in your remote control or in your phone: it makes the phone work and gives it the power so that when you press the buttons, they do something. Likewise, your statue will work for you only if she is charged!

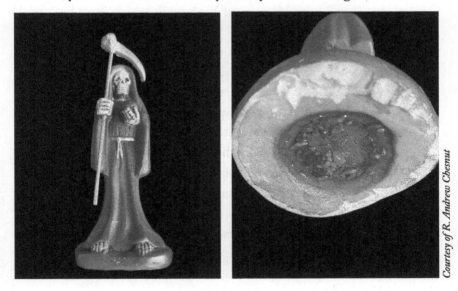

Courtesy of R. Andrew Chesnut

Small statue, with *carga* consisting of seeds at the base. The larger the statue, the more complex and bigger the *carga*.

There are exceptions to this rule. Some statues are not charged, as this is not necessary. For example, statues made of wood generally do not have *una carga*. They do not need it. A *curandera* explained it to me this way, "Santa Muerte statues made of wood are known to be powerful because wood conducts puissant forces from the earth, through the tree from its roots up to its outer branches, and that wood emanates earth energy, sending that energy from deep below the earth into your statue."

Wooden statues are usually handmade and thus have been made with care, potentially by artists, shamans, or Indigenous artisans who will further add layers of power in carving la Santa Muerte from a carefully selected piece of wood in a labor of love that speaks to their deep devotion to death. Of course, wooden statues are also cherished family heirlooms and last far longer than those made of resin and are passed down through many generations. The most ancient and venerated statues of Most Holy Death are made of wood, such as that owned by the Cruz family of Tepatepec, Hidalgo, Mexico. Their statue is two hundred years old and has been passed down through their family from at least the 19th century. Even older than this one is the ancient wooden skeletal figure with a crown and scythe from Oaxaca, now kept in the Museum of Yanhuitlán, which dates back to the 17th century.

Another exception to the rule of always having a *carga* in your statue pertains to effigies made of stone, quartz, and rock. Artisans in Mexico shape images of Saint Death in natural materials, such as black obsidian and other stones, like those hewn from pink volcanic rock known as *cantera rosa*. Many beautiful examples can be found at the splendid shrine of *Casa de la Santa Muerte* (House of Santa Muerte) chapel in Santa Ana Chapitiro, Michoacan. These rock and stone statues have no *carga* as they do not require it. They are charged already, given that they are made from a material that conducts intensely.

Courtesy of R. Andrew Chesnut

Wooden Oaxacan statue of Santa Muerte dating back to the 17th century

Stone and rock are supremely strong and solid, and will bring that strength to your *brujeria* and ritual work. They channel energy in unadulterated form from deep within the earth's core. Such materials exude power and vigor.

Although wooden statues may be obtained online, in general those made of stone or rock are unique and often can be purchased only in special locations, primarily in Mexico. The advantage of stone statues is their longevity and durability. If you are fortunate enough to have a concealed yard or other outdoor space to worship in, this is an ideal place to establish an altar with a stone statue. Working outside with Santa Muerte, in particular, nocturnally, directly in contact with the energy of the earth, the breath of the wind, while bathed in the rays of the moon and showered with cascades of stars, will empower your work intensely, allowing for a deep bond with Death.

Aside from my *curandera* friend in Atoyac River, who has a beautiful riverside shrine, I once met a *bruja* with Olmec ancestry who took understandable pride in her magnificent outdoor Holy Death shrine, right next to a *panteon*, as they call a cemetery in Spanish. Her shrine has a pond, overlooked by a stunning statue of la Santísima Muerte, and innumerable other statuettes are positioned in the grounds. These statues of all colors are placed in alignment with the space of each area so that they imbue each area with a different mystique. The *curandera* told me she worked far more freely outdoors, channeling the elements around

her, such as wind and air, as well as the illumination of the moon to infuse her work fully in the fundamental energies of our earth that the skeleton saint thrives upon. At night, on a new moon, I have seen Santa Muerte's shadow emerge from the pond and wander around her garden, disappearing into the cemetery next door to walk among the spirits of the dead whose souls belong to her.

Bone statues, rare and hard to come by, require no *carga* and are incredibly powerful. After all, they are made of the Bone Mother's—as

Courtesy of R. Andrew Chesnut

Santa Muerte hewn from volcanic rock at the Casa de la Santa Muerte chapel in Michoacan

Santa Muerte is sometimes dubbed—intrinsic element: collagen and minerals intricately woven in an organic matrix. Bone statues are generally made of cow bones, occasionally pig bones, and they are an excellent choice for any devotee, allowing you to connect directly with Death. Nevertheless, before you purchase a statue made from bone, it is crucial to verify that you are not buying human bone. Should the person have died a tragic death of unnatural causes, this will bring intense negativity into your spiritual work, and your home and life will be haunted by that person's pain and suffering. Worse still, should the person have been evil in their life, you will bring malevolence and destruction into your home, and this may bring all manner of ill fortune to you, your loved ones, and your career.

Size

Size is an important consideration for all devotees, but bigger is not better. The size you choose depends on how large your altar space is, as well as what you can afford, combined with your needs. But also keep in mind your lifestyle. In Mexico, the devotees I know generally keep one or more medium-size statues at home, or a large one if they are more affluent, but those who travel frequently have small statues for that very purpose. Keep in mind that, because of their size, little statues have less *carga* than large ones, but this does not make them less effective.

Small statues are essential during travel. Just because you are away from home does not mean that prayer, ritual, and devotion to death take a break or end. Your dedication to Santa Muerte, even when you are a million miles from home, will ensure success in all your ventures. After all, it is often the case that when we are away from the security of our home, we need our Deathly Mother the most. Whether it is a long road trip down a dangerous highway, visiting a sick family member whose health we are worried about, or traveling for work to seal a deal or in the hopes of acing that job interview, or even going on that first vacation with that hot new lover, these are all occasions when you may need the support of Santa Muerte to guarantee your endeavors are successful.

A *curandero* friend of mine who is from the northern state of Tabasco often travels across Mexico, as far south as Acapulco, to dispense healing. In his peregrinations, he always brings numerous small statues with him. They protect him on the road, and upon arrival in his lodgings, he erects a mini altar, giving whatever offerings he can obtain, such as a glass of water, a piece of fruit, candy, and a glass of whatever alcoholic libation he is able to secure. I have followed his procedure during long or worrisome journeys. I have found that, upon arrival, setting up a small altar—even if it contains but one or two statuettes and merely a few offerings—is an excellent way to connect with Most Holy Death and find comfort, solace, and even a feeling of home through spiritual connection with her wherever I may be.

Such small figurines are also useful for perilous everyday situations, and many of my friends in Mexico carry *la Madrina* around with them during difficult or dangerous times. It is recommended you do so too. For example, truck drivers often have a small effigy with them on the dashboard, as long hours of driving on hairpin bends means they need Santa's protection to avoid accidents. One follower of Holy Death told me he hid his effigy of a green Santa Muerte of justice in his pocket when he had to go to court and defend himself. Every time he felt anxious, he reached in and touched the familiar form of la Justiciera. She comforted him and kept him calm throughout the process. Eventually, he was acquitted.

Another female devotee would often carry a black statue, la Niña Negra, with her for protection when she returned late at night from her job at a local bar and had to walk home alone along treacherous empty streets that hid rapists, muggers, and murderers in their shadowy corners. She told me that la Niña Negra always protected her, and nothing had ever happened to her. Once, she recounted, a dangerous group of thugs was walking toward her threateningly with switch blades in hand and crazy eyes. She clutched her Santa Muerte statue in her purse and recited a small prayer in her head. In response, the Powerful Lady at that very next moment created a distraction for them. The thugs were sidetracked by two cars driving by with blaring music whose occupants jeered and hollered at the gangsters. She managed to dart down a side street away from their gaze and reach her home.

These are just a few examples of why small statues are useful, and they illustrate how you can use mini Muerte statues in tricky everyday situations to bless your endeavors and ensure your safety. Even a trip to the beach or to the forest can become an opportunity to bless a small statue in a babbling brook or the waves of the ocean and perform an impromptu ritual to honor Santa Muerte. Indeed, some of the most accomplished shamans of Santa Muerte that I know, or devoted followers, bring their statues with them on trips into nature to suffuse their statues with the potent, vibrant energy of Mother Earth and the elements.

Medium and large statues are impressive, and the larger they are, the more presence they have. The ideal for many devotees is a life-size statue, but most of us can ill afford the hefty price tag of one this size, nor do we have the space for such a large effigy, especially if we need to hide our devotion to Death from gossipmongers and judgmental family members.

In my own personal practice, I have found medium-size statues are an excellent choice for a home altar. This size allows you to make a good connection with la Santa, and by awakening, naming, and caring for the statue as you would any member of your family, you will form a bond with her. I recommend not only prayer to your statue, but as people do in Mexico, talking to her like you would any family member; additionally, as you would before any deity, being humble and kneeling prostrate before her during ritual and prayer. Respect, humility, and care are key ingredients in building a relationship.

The neophyte should know that any statue of Santa Muerte is a repository for her spirit. This is the way in which Most Holy Death comes to you, as her spirit will flow into the statue—that is, if she is happy, and you have welcomed her in the correct manner. This will bless your ventures. Therefore, making offerings to her, plus cleansing the altar regularly and the statue itself are important. Of course, it takes time to form that bond, but with care and love, you should be rewarded. Over time, she will come to you in dreams and communicate with you with increasing frequency and depth through your altar and omens.

Also important in working with Santa Muerte through her effigy is to pay attention to the statue as you would any person in your household. You would not ignore whether a friend liked the meal you served them or the gift you gave them. The same is true of the Powerful Lady: you must pay attention to her likes and dislikes and observe her, taking note of her needs and desires. Her statue will communicate to you whether it is through movements, gestures, occurrences around the altar and in your house, or facial expressions. On my altar, I have witnessed my main effigy smile at me when she is pleased with an offering. Likewise, my statue sometimes moves to let me know she is present. Recently, upon the completion of an elaborate ritual to her, a green stone was thrown at my feet from my altar. Given the nature of my petition, I knew she had heard my request. Not long thereafter I had significant news regarding the matter I had petitioned her for. Santa Muerte shows many emotions, just as we do, and the altar is where they are most often directly made known.

A devotee I know related to me that her Holy Death statue had shown anger when she was accidentally mistreated. Indeed, Santa Muerte, like any person, may be offended and upset by certain actions. The devotee told me that her brother had taken her statue outside to smoke a cigarette with her. On the way, unnoticed by him as he transported the statue outdoors, a necklace that she had gifted her effigy to thank the Bone Mother for a miracle had fallen off la Santa onto the dirt in the yard. Later that day, things started to go wrong. Her mobile phone started crashing constantly, and things began falling off the shelves. That night she could barely sleep. A violent wind kept howling outside, and something seemed to be banging at her window.

The following morning when she woke up and went to say good morning to la Santa, the statue was turned away from her. When she put the statue back in place, she saw an angry scowl on the folk saint's face but did not understand why. She paid close attention, and it was then that she noticed that the beautiful necklace she had bought for *la Niña* was missing from her statue. She retraced her brother's steps and found it lying in the dirt outside. She washed and cleansed it spiritually and placed it around her Santa's bony neck. Thereafter, her phone started working again, things stopped falling off shelves, the wind died down, and the sun shone through an open window beaming down on the altar. La Santa was smiling again. This is but one such story of many I have heard, and I have related its contents so that, as a neophyte, you are aware of the importance of paying attention to your Holy Death statues and reading the signs they present.

Statue Poses and Forms

In Mexico, Santa Muerte statues exist in many different styles. Outside of the country, people are largely unfamiliar with the many distinct poses or how they are to be used. The following sections teach you the secrets of the poses.

Standing

The standing pose is the most ubiquitous and well-known form of *la Madrina*. In her standing pose, Holy Death appears upright, her body covered in a long tunic that extends down to her bony feet. In her hands, she generally has a scythe, the scales of justice, sometimes a book, or even a lantern. She often is accompanied by an owl, which acts as her messenger. These different attributes and the powers related to them will be described later in this chapter. In her standing pose, Santa Muerte's full force, sanctity, and splendor are visible. This statue is multipurpose and recommended to the neophyte, for it can be used in any petition and on any altar. In her standing form, she is

active, ready to pounce on intruders and slash down with her scythe. For those who need protection and to be guarded by death's powerful hand from malevolent forces, this statue is the best choice. For those who need rapid action and miracles, this is also an excellent choice. This standing statue is a favorite among devotees, for Santa Muerte will, using the statue as her vessel, come through on any petition in this form.

Enthroned

In her enthroned pose, Santa Muerte sits majestically and straight-backed, usually on a large, imposing, and often ornate throne. Enthroned, she displays her celestial sovereignty as most powerful Queen of Death. In this pose, she generally wields a huge scythe in her right hand; and in her left, a globe, a lantern, an hourglass, or the scales of justice. Sometimes an owl accompanies her, often above her begowned shoulder or at her osseous toes. Also at her skeletal feet are countless skulls, depicting her dominion over death. Sometimes coins may also be below her, signifying her ability to help you reap riches. In some statues I have seen, the saint of death's left foot rests atop the globe, as if it were but a stool for her bony toes. This position demonstrates her absolute dominion not only over death but also everything on this earth, whose life only she has the power to take.

Enthroned, she oozes power at its zenith, the wisdom that only a primeval being thousands of years dead can possess. When holding the scales of justice, she exemplifies her strength as judge, jury, and executioner who can swing the scales in your favor or against you or your enemies. When holding the scales of justice upon her throne, she is ideal for those who need to call on her power for an immovable issue, for guidance in difficult matters, or for legal troubles. Finally, this statue is excellent for those who want to come into their full power and need strength from the Bone Mother to help them leave a difficult situation such as a bad job, a violent relationship, or another situation in which they are mistreated and undervalued. This statue is for those who want to move into a space of power, of leadership, and who need Holy Death's support to teach them how to take what life has to offer. Queen Death will show you how to take command and become the leader of your own life.

Open Armed

In her open-armed pose, Santa Muerte stands upright, usually with her hands empty. Sometimes they may contain a scythe and/or a globe. This pose was made famous across Mexico by Jonathan Legaria Vargas, better known as Comandante Pantera. In the folk saint's honor, he built the largest statue of Holy Death in the world in Tultitlan (on the outskirts of

Mexico City) and launched the Temple of Santa Muerte International (SMI). This immense effigy consists of an open-armed statue of the skeleton saint, measuring 72 feet high. El Comandante was gunned down in 2008 not far from the effigy, but his mother, Enriqueta Vargas, took the reins. She prayed avidly to Santa Muerte to avenge her son's death, promising that if la Madrina came through, she would make her name known across the land. Enriqueta states that Holy Death swung her scythe down with mighty fury upon her son's killers. To thank la Santísima Muerte, Enriqueta, with great determination and unparalleled charisma, significantly expanded SMI and established churches dedicated to preaching death across the Americas. After her death from cancer in 2018, her daughter Kristhel Legaria Vargas took over. Nevertheless, to this day this statue stands staring defiantly over those who cower below in her deathly shadow.

As this effigy is modeled on the largest statue of the Powerful Lady in the world, this pose has been made famous. Defense, benevolence, and receptivity are the attributes associated with open-armed Santa Muerte. Her open arms signify her acceptance of all devotees regardless of race, class, sexual orientation, or lifestyle choices. We are all children of death, for she comes to us all. Her open arms also allow for receptivity, and thus in petitions where you wish to receive more of anything—be it tangible, such as money and goods, or intangible, such as love and power—this is an ideal statue. Also in this pose, the Lady of the Shadows stands ready to defend you and keep harm at bay. If you have a garden or other outdoor space by your home, you would do well to place a large open-armed statue of la Santa in it so that she may keep your space safe from intruders and unwanted visitors, while drawing in good energy, money, and other positive elements into your home.

Pregnant Santa Muerte

In this statue, Santa Muerte is heavily pregnant. The fetus inside is often visible thanks to translucent resin through which a curled-up, prenatal babe can be seen in her womb. This effigy features her with her right hand wielding her scythe and the left typically tenderly touching her embryo. Sometimes this image depicts the skeleton saint as half living and half dead, with one side of her full and fleshy and the other half as skull and bones. She may also display the pendulous breasts of pregnancy. This statue represents not only Santa Muerte's power over death but also her absolute puissance as she who brings life. This effigy is the obvious choice for anyone who wishes to have a baby, as in this guise Most Holy Death will bring life to the empty womb. Men who wish to help their partners get pregnant or women who wish to have a baby would be advised to use this statue in conjunction with the prayers and rituals outlined in chapter six.

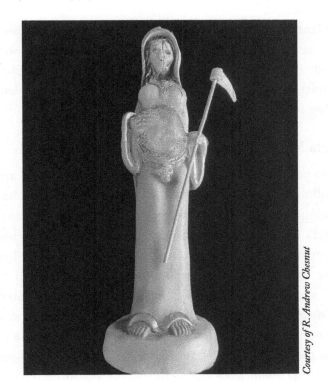

Many women in Mexico have this statue, and the fecund figure is frequently found on female-owned altars. Some women have even created beautiful fertility niches, and you may wish to do so too, in alignment with some of the ideas that follow. One of the most beautiful examples I have seen contained a plethora of pregnant Santa Muerte statues, both large and small, around a large bowl of water that looked like a serene lake and was surrounded by flowers and leafy, fertile plants. The devotee's offerings consisted of things evocative of babies such as baby wipes, soft toys, and healthy foods babies can eat, such as bananas. Her gifts also comprised those I would recommend to you for conceiving a baby, items that were round like the womb in its burgeoning state, such as buns, a watermelon, or that resembled the uterus, like avocados. This statue exists in many colors, such as pink, white, red, mauve, and the seven-colored figurines, which are all excellent choices. I have seen it in black, which is not a color I would recommend for pregnancy requests, given its association with darker magic.

Pregnant Bone Mother is also an excellent statue for someone who is starting a new project and feels full of fresh ideas, brimming with creativity or ready to commence a new business venture. With regular prayer to her and offerings, she will help you grow the seed you have planted into a burgeoning tree.

Santa Muerte with Babe in Arms or Children at Her Feet

Related to pregnant Santa Muerte is the skeleton saint who appears lovingly cradling a baby in her bony arms or with her osseous hands softly safeguarding small children at her feet. In this pose she frequently appears with angel's wings, which may be juxtaposed to eyes that burn red with wrath, symbolizing both her absolute love as a nurturing mother to small, vulnerable children and her deadly determination to stop at nothing to keep evil away from them. This effigy is the ideal choice for those who need *la Madrina* to look after their little ones. Whether it is sickness that plagues your child, or a violent partner whom you fear will hurt them, or danger on the streets that poses a risk to them, in her job as Bone Mother, she will shelter them from harm. This statue would be the ideal one to use in conjunction with the prayer for protection of children featured in chapter six. Alongside prayers, it is recommended you light white candles, but when strong protection is needed, a black candle alongside this is recommended. A red candle, signifying your love for your children, forming a trio of black, white, and red is a powerful way to petition la Santa for their safety.

Santa Muerte Holding Jesus

Santa Muerte holding Jesus conveys many messages. First, she reminds us that in Mexico, despite the Church's condemnation of the skeleton saint, most devotees consider her Catholic. As is evident from the prayers in chapter six, sometimes permission is sought from God to work with Santa Muerte, or the dual powers of Death herself and God are invoked. From a theological point of view, this statue reminds us that Holy Death took Jesus's life and that his demise was necessary so he could atone and be resurrected, his body thus transformed into a spiritual, divine entity. While in Catholic theology, according to Paul, this is how Death lost her bitter bite and became the servant of God and humankind, in Mexico this is not necessarily the way devotees see the relationship between Jesus and Santa Muerte. Maternal and powerful, the Bone Mother supports a supine Jesus, depicting that, rather than a servant, she is even more powerful than God. Death claims all, and even took Jesus's life.

Iconographically, the pose derives from la Pietà, a Renaissance sculpture by Michelangelo Buonarroti, which depicts the body of Jesus on the lap of his mother Mary after the Crucifixion. But in this version, Santa Muerte replaces Mary as the ultimate maternal figure. This statue is well suited for those who have experienced much suffering and need to call on la Santísima Muerte's feminine strength in the context of great trials and tribulations. Whether tormented by physical or mental pain, or even crippling addictions, this effigy will channel the Bone Mother's healing, compassionate, and caring energies and bring them to your home. Pray to her for help and healing, and she will listen to you as any mother would, and provide strength, love, and miracles to allow you to get through any difficult period in your life. For help with healing, mauve, white, and yellow candles are ideal.

Santa Muerte Astride a Horse

The pose of Santa Muerte astride a horse is available in some esoteric stores. I have seen her on only one altar, and her striking figure is hard to forget. The owner of the altar was a dangerous-looking man who had a shop selling everyday wares in a hazardous neighborhood in Pachuca, Hidalgo. At the back of his store, on a shelf in a shadowy corner, he had placed this figure surrounded by black candles and offerings of all kinds, including ebony dahlias, dollars, tequila, and tobacco. Flying threateningly out from the darkness, astride her rearing horse, the Skeleton Saint stunned me and warned me that she was ready to strike down whosoever stepped too far. I was told by locals that by day the owner ran that store, but by night he was a narco, and that the backroom of his shop served as a known locale for hoarding drugs and weapons. Evidently, Santa Muerte stood on guard warning people not to step any further nor mess with the owner of the establishment.

This statue features Holy Death riding on a galloping stallion with scythe in hand, her long gown flowing behind her, ready to reap the souls of those she encounters. In terms of iconography, this effigy derives from the story of the four horsemen of the apocalypse mentioned in the Book of Revelations. In this Christian text, which speaks of the End Time, or doomsday, the fourth horseman represents death. Christian art has portrayed this figure as riding a pale horse, carrying a hefty sword, scythe, or other trenchant implement. In the Book of Revelations, also known as the Apocalypse of John, and attributed to John of Patmos, Death is called Θάνατος and the Greek word for plague is θανάτῳ, evidently a variation of Θάνατος, indicating a profound connection between the fourth horseman and plague. Such a connection between plague and death is food for thought during the spread of the coronavirus, when the Saint of Death has twelve million followers during the time of the pandemic, many of whom have been affected especially financially, mentally, and possibly physically by the context of the pandemic.

Astride her horse, Holy Death is in her most active and lethal pose, ready for battle, and to deliver instant death. This effigy is for those who are on the offensive, especially those seeking to tap into the power of death to hex their enemies or otherwise create deadly devastation through *brujeria*. A black statue in this pose for ultimate efficacy in cursing would be most efficient. It may be that you do not want to hex anyone, but you do want the Bone Mother to do her worst to any enemies should they assault you or trespass, whether physically or energetically. You can rely on *la Madrina* in this pose to give you unwavering, ferocious protection and to use her scythe to cut down anyone who stands in your way. If you need to return evil to the sender, this is also the ideal statue, and it is recommended you light a "reversible" candle, which is both black and red (see chapter five, "Colors and Candles").

If you do wish to hex someone, placing their photo below this statue, with their eyes crossed out in black, following the recitation of an imprecation to harm your enemies, as can be found in chapter six, would be advisable. You should also follow the instructions for using a black candle. You are warned to do this at your own peril. Santa Muerte, especially *la Niña Negra* (Santa Muerte in her black form), does not take hexes lightly, so you must remember that any malevolent magic you do unto others may be returned to you if and when la Santísima Muerte sees fit. You will also have to serve her dutifully, and should you fail to thank her, she will take out her immense rage on you. The dark side of the Powerful Lady is her most formidable and forceful form but also her most deadly and for this reason must be treated with the utmost respect and caution.

Santa Muerte Incarnate

A more recent version of Santa Muerte is known as *la Encarnada*, or the Incarnate One; sometimes she is called *doble cara*, or dual/double face. While she is not as popular as more common figures, such as the standing Santa Muerte figure, I have nevertheless seen her across Mexico, including on sale in Doña Queta's store, which adjoins her world-famous Holy Death shrine in Tepito. Young people, in particular, appear to be drawn to this effigy. She is similar to the design that David Romo attempted to popularize before his incarceration for kidnapping and other crimes. Romo was the Archbishop of *La Iglesia Católica Tradicionalista mexicana-estadounidense*, sometimes known as the Traditionalist Mexico–USA Tridentine Catholic Church, which broke away from the Vatican when Romo began to include the Powerful Lady within his services. The figure was met with controversy, as the incarnate, voluptuous figure of Santa Muerte was based on his wife and was rather too provocative for those who preferred to see the skeleton saint as dead rather than drop-dead sexy.

In this form, the skeleton saint is no longer bony but featured in fleshy form, usually with generous curves and plunging necklines, dressed in a long gown replete with a bodice or even sometimes a corset. The folk saint is often depicted with dual or double-face. One side is that of a living woman, with an attractive half-face and long dark locks, whereas the other side depicts a defleshed skull. This dual face symbolizes her powers over both life and death and, as devotees have explained to me, the fact that she can bring both good and bad. The style is syncretic, just like Santa Muerte's origins, as it is influenced not only by Memento Mori and Vanitas art from Europe, such as that of Tomás Mondragón and his *Alegoría de La Muerte*, but also from Indigenous Mexican art. In Mexico, pre-Columbian Tarascan pottery, for example, displayed imagery of the *doble cara*, or dual face of both life and death.

The young, buxom figure also hearkens, as I was told by a wise woman and witch, to one of the origin tales of the folk saint. A Santa Muerte sorceress recounted it to me in this manner, although many variants exist:

· · · · · ❈ · · · · ·

It is said that once upon a time, Holy Death was a young, beautiful woman, just like the figure in the statue. She was engaged to be married to a young man. On the day of her wedding, she went to the church dressed in purest white. She waited for hours for her fiancé, but the young man never came. He jilted her at the altar. Ashamed, crying, and heartbroken, she no longer wanted to be on this earth and decided to take her own life, but upon dying and reaching the heavens, she was declined entry by God. He told her that her soul was so pure and her heart so good that she must stay on earth to take care of the ailing, the poor, the wounded, the wretched, the lost, and the broken-hearted, and granted her unique powers of both life and death so that she would be able to do this work. She also decided to use her powers to punish those who hurt others.

· · · · · ❈ · · · · ·

This statue in Mexico, along with Santa Muerte as a bride (see the next section), is thus often called on by those who are broken-hearted to mend the hurt and find a new loved one. The statue is also used by those who wish to ignite passion in their lives. Love, sexual, and passion petitions are popular with this statue, which often features in red, white, pink, or seven colors. For love and sex, the red candle is the obvious choice. I have seen other devotees use the statue for more general petitions, and some call on the gold version of this statue to ask for riches and opulence.

Also, to be taken into consideration is that in Mexico some men become Holy Death's betrothed, marrying her or becoming her loyal boyfriend. They give her all the gifts associated with courtship, from roses to chocolates and even jewelry and perfume. However, it is important to understand that this relationship will only ever be one-sided, for the Powerful Lady belongs to no man, and devotees will tell you that indeed she belongs to no one at all; not even God himself has power over la Santa, although she works with him, as is evident from the prayers in chapter six. However, any man may choose to love her as he would a wife and dedicate himself to her. For this purpose, this effigy is ideal. If you are a single man who wishes to enter into a deep, loving relationship with Santa Muerte, this image is ideal for you. She will comfort you, look after you, and aid you if you are good to her. It is advised that you gift her all the sweet treats, flowers, and other such gifts that you would any girlfriend, fiancée, or wife.

I have also seen revealing versions of this statue in which Most Holy Death is scantily clad, exposing much skin, rotund bust, and silky leg. The seductive version of this figurine is popular with members of the cartel, especially younger men, and the statue stems from the narco-aesthetic. Many rich drug dealers keep young girlfriends or wives, whom they encourage to undergo plastic surgery to enlarge their body parts to preternatural proportions. It should be remembered that Mexico is number three in the world in the number of plastic surgeries. Such operations remain the purview of the rich, and narcos influence this industry with extreme and unrealistic aesthetic desires that seem to have also shaped the stylistics of the seductive Santa Muerte statue.

Death as Bride

Statues of Santa Muerte dressed as a bride are hard to buy. In most part, devotees dress their own effigies, especially larger ones, in a bridal gown, with a veil and often a tiara, with a posy bouquet in her bony hand, as if she were about to walk down the aisle. This ivory-white matrimonial garb is usually hand-made by those followers who are skilled in sewing, or devotees may pay someone to create such bridal apparel for their statue. Of course, dressed as a bride, the statue is petitioned by those who seek a committed, loyal, loving life partner and to be married as soon as possible. White flowers are the perfect present for the skeleton saint in her bridal apparel, representing marriage, but pink roses are also gifted in such a setting. Chocolates, candy, and other sweet treats, such as honey and cinnamon, which represent sweetness and warmth but also mimic the gifts you would give someone you were courting, are the ideal offerings. If you are longing to meet your soul mate and be wed, it is recommended that you buy or create a Santa Muerte in a bridal gown and pray to her regularly, lighting white, pink, and red candles.

Angel of Death

In her form as the Angel of Death, Santa Muerte always appears with magnificent, plumed, angel wings that are spread out above her flowing gown. This effigy is usually white, silver, or gold, although I have seen black statues. The wings signify her celestial energy as Angel of Death, who collects but also comforts souls upon their passing. In this form, the skeleton saint is benevolent and at her most pure, channeling the most bounteous and beautiful energy from the heavens above. This image is ideal for those who need the Bone Mother as a guardian angel in their life, watching over them, protecting them as well as their family, and sending them blessings. This effigy is also ideal for those who have lost a beloved, for through Santa Muerte you can talk to your dearly departed and be sure they are safe within her bony embrace and watching over you from heaven. To connect with the Angel of Death, you should light white, silver, and even gold candles if you are suffering monetarily.

Aztec Death, Indigenous Muerte

Many have told me that Aztec Death, or Indigenous Muerte, is only for the experienced due to her potency and fickleness. In particular, this statue is known for her trickster spirit and powerful magical abilities of *brujeria*. In Mesoamerican mythology, tricksters are dangerous, cunning, and powerful figures, who, while supremely spiritual and imbued with magic, may also use this to create calamity, distort sight and sound, and otherwise inveigle. They love to humiliate and embarrass humans and other deities, in particular through the realm of the senses and the carnal. In this vein, while Aztec Muerte may grant you great favors, she can also trick you and bring mishaps to you that serve as a lesson, especially to the ego.

Courtesy of R. Andrew Chesnut

She commands ancient powers of death that date back thousands of years to pre-Hispanic Mexico and its native peoples. Dressed in a plumed Aztec-style headdress, Holy Death in this form features elements of Amerindian iconography, sometimes corn emblems and other such symbology. Some devotees state that the skeleton saint is Aztec in origin, deriving from Mictecacihuatl, the Goddess of Death, and her husband Mictlantecuhtli. However, others will attribute different origins to her depending on the region. Indigenous-style statues often feature Maya elements intermixed with Aztec and even other Amerindian symbols and glyphs. Of course, the Maya worshiped death deities also, as did many other Indigenous Mexican peoples, such as the Mixtec, Tarascans, Totonacos, and Zapotec. Thus, this statue reflects ancient devotion to death through its interplay of Amerindian elements and is the most mystical of all. As such, this manifestation of Santa Muerte is a conduit for atavistic, thanatic forces and can be used to tap into those powers in order to explore arcane questions and acquire the vital energy of primeval death. Such an effigy can also be used to speak to archaic ancestors and explore esoteric mysteries by appealing directly to ancient sources of power and the spirits of the dead. It should never be named anything but an Indigenous-type name; otherwise, this would be a mark of disrespect.

The Maya *curandero* I know, who lives alone in the depths of the jungle, works only with an Indigenous effigy of death. He does so to honor the ancient origins of Santa Muerte and his own pre-Hispanic bloodline. In trances, he conducts ritual bloodletting to Santa Muerte and summons his ancestral spirits from Xibalba, the underworld, whom he tells me come up through the *cenote* by his shrine every full moon to speak to him through Holy Death.

Some of the Indigenous *curanderos* I know are fond of working with *la Azteca*, although not all see her as Aztec but ascribe other Indigenous origins to her. Many such *curanderos* possess incredible ethnopharmacological knowledge of plants and herbs that has been passed down through generations. They work with the old ways, such as divining through corn kernels and curing with plants and unique secrets of *brujeria* known only to them. Some connect with *la Azteca* and other aspects of Santa Muerte through entheogens. I detail only those I have knowledge of. Psilocybin mushrooms and sage of the diviner (*hoja de la pastora* or *ska Maria pastora*) are the tools of the Mazatec and Zapotec shamans of Oaxaca. They have been used for healing, cleansing, and divining for thousands of years. One such important mushroom is *psilocybe zapotecorum*, named for the Zapotec and known locally as *badao zoo*, which means drunk god, while in Nahuatl it is called *teotlacuilnanácatl*, which means the sacred mushroom that paints through color figures, as it produces vivid hallucinations. Another entheogen is the Mexican prickly poppy, *argemone Mexicana*, which can alter consciousness when smoked. The Aztecs honored the plant as the "food of the dead" during their reign, believing souls refreshed themselves on it in the realm of the dead. *Heimia salicifolia*, known as the "Herb of the spirits" (*hierba de los espiritus*), is an auditory hallucinogen altering your hearing so that you perceive sounds far away and the whispers of spirits. It also allows for astral travel and lucid dreaming. Mexican shamans use it to connect with divine spirits and receive messages, including those from Santa Muerte. Other herbs may be used not only with *la Azteca* but also in general to connect with Santa Muerte and the astral realms in dreams. I recommend mugwort, valerian, and in particular, Mexican calea or calea zacatechichi, also known as bitter-grass or Aztec Dream Grass.

Ideal offerings to connect with Santa Muerte in her most antediluvian form are those that have been consumed for thousands of years in Mexico: corn, tortillas, chocolate, avocados, guacamole, pecans, pumpkin seeds, mole, aloe leaves, and pulque. Burn copal for her. She also likes tobacco and *cempasuchil* (yellow marigold flowers).

Final Thoughts on Pose and Form

As a final note, there is no right or wrong choice in your selection of statue. Every devotee has their own motivations and attractions to different statues, even if so-called Aztec Death is said to be the most difficult to work with and not for the neophyte, given that it takes time and demonstrations of utter respect to be permitted to work with her. But be aware that your budget is not of concern. In Mexico, where devotees often cannot afford to buy more than one or two statues, the most simple effigy may serve to ask for love, protection, health, wealth, and much more. Ultimately, what you are drawn to will guide you through your intuition. And most of all, it is your faith, regular prayer, and devotion that will wield results, not the largesse, opulence, or high price tag of your statue.

While it is interesting to think about iconography, for devotees in Mexico, such theological considerations are rarely pondered. Only some *curanderos* and Santa Muerte leaders tend to consider the deeper, dogmatic meanings and how to benefit from the greater secrets they may hold. For those living on less than a dollar a day, often in the midst of drug wars, or even as soldiers involved in incessant narco-battles, there is little time for contemplation; rather, immediate action and miracles are what is required from Holy Death. Indeed, if Santa Muerte is the most popular folk saint in Mexico, one of the many reasons is her reputation for rapidly answering prayers and empowering spells to bring forth miracles. This book will give you the keys to bring her efficacy into your life.

Ritual to Awaken Your Statues and Cleansing Ritual

Evil spirits can enter into any statue at any time. This is why it is important to cleanse your effigies—not only upon receiving them for the first time but also regularly: at least once per month. The type of cleansing deemed requisite depends on the level of spiritual pollution detected. It is usually sufficient to just waft incense and/or tobacco smoke over your effigies if you believe them to be free of deep negative energies, but a cleansing should be more thorough and consist of herbal bathing and washing if you sense that evil spirits or energies are present or that someone has been attacking you. Some statues can be possessed by malevolent forces, and it is recommended that statues be cleansed and, if possible, moon-bathed at least every month to ensure they are freed of all ill energies.

A statue bought in a store may have been touched by innumerable people with many different energies and some, perhaps with tainted intentions, who have unknowingly infused them into the statue. That is why on bringing your purchased or gifted statue home, before you place her on the altar, the first thing to do is to "awaken" her, as they call it in Mexico, and cleanse her. Most *curanderos* and *brujos* like to do this using an herbal elixir and tobacco. I recommend their technique above others I have heard of. This technique consists of bathing Santa Muerte with an infusion of herbs in water.

The first step is to bathe and cleanse yourself. In Mexico, this is known as *un baño* (a bath), and it consists of washing yourself, often with specific herbs to cleanse yourself of psychic pollution. The bath will ensure you are clean and free of negative energy before commencing. You can have a simple shower, focusing on removing cosmic grime and bad energy, but if you feel you are carrying a highly negative charge, you may wish to use Santa Muerte soap (if you have it) and any of the herbal recipes described later to bathe not only Most Holy Death but also yourself. If this is the case, you will need to double or triple the ingredients, depending on your stature and the size of and number of your statues. After showering, do *una limpia* (spiritual cleanse) with incense. Often known as *un sahumerio*, an incense bath is wafting the smoke of incense or tobacco all over yourself, and possibly your house, to lift away negative energies. To bathe la Santa, you should create the herbal potion detailed later; as stated, you may also bathe yourself in this potion. If you need to cleanse yourself of heavy energy, in Mexico and some botanicas outside of the country, Santa Muerte lotions, ritual bath salts, and even seven-day bath kits are sold for the purposes of cleansing. Some are of excellent quality and contain real herbs, whereas others contain artificial fragrances and smell unpleasant. If you're in doubt whether a product is of good quality or not, it is preferable to brew your own herbs, as the most powerful witches and healers of Mexico do.

To brew your purifying water—in the more traditional way—to cleanse and awaken your Santa Muerte statue, pour your mixture of herbs into water and boil until the liquid has taken on the hue, aroma, and powers of the plants. Different *brujos* have recommended distinct recipes to me, and I suggest you refer to the "Optional *Hierbateria* (Herbal Items)" section in chapter three to select the herbs according to your needs. Although dried herbs are best for burning as incense, for the purposes of making the herbal bathing potion, fresh herbs are best if you can obtain them or grow them. However, if you cannot obtain fresh, dried herbs also work well, and the Powerful Lady understands that it is not always easy to get fresh herbs! As to the water you use, most devotees use plain tap water. However, if you are fortunate enough to be able obtain sea or river water or to collect rain, these are superlative choices as these liquids come from nature and will bring the sea or sky blessings into your spiritual work. You may also make full moon water, as detailed in "Times of Day and Night to Work with Santa Muerte."

Many *curanderos* and *brujos* in Mexico use a mixture of these basic herbs, which are the three sisters of cleansing: rosemary, rue, and basil. Sometimes one of these is swapped with sage. Rosemary, rue, and basil are the ultimate trio for multipurpose work, and can be boiled together for cleansing and awakening any statue and for cleansing yourself. Rue is key in cleansing recipes; it is potentially an abortifacient, so pregnant women or those seeking to conceive must avoid contact. A more pungent option that I was told to use by a *curandera* when I felt dark and negative energy was afflicting me, or severe illness sent by witchcraft, is simply garlic boiled in a pot with water and used to wash yourself and your statue.

In urban spaces, devotees frequently prefer to buy bottled colognes and flower waters for their cleanses, rather than brew up herbs that may be more difficult to obtain. They use *siete machos* mixed with water; sometimes rosewater (*agua de rosas*) is added for love, and orange blossom water such as *Agua de Colonia flor de naranja*, for tranquility and harmony. Many use Florida water, known in Spanish as *agua de Florida*. Lotions may be used, such as *locion Santa Muerte*. For the busy devotee, or the one who has difficulty obtaining herbs, the flower waters and colognes are a good choice. While I sometimes use perfumes such as *siete machos* when in a hurry, I have found the use of pure herbal waters is profoundly therapeutic and potent. Herbal water is a superior offering because it is prepared with your energy, care, and love, not bought in a bottle made in a factory. Of course, you must decide what suits you best. However, you should note that herbal work—that is to say, choosing and brewing herbs—is spell work, *brujeria*, and if prayers are chanted and intentions are focused into the bubbling herbal waters as you prepare them, these will bring additional power and magic to your altar. Additionally, for those who are more thrifty or who like to grow their own herbs or collect them in nature, as some of the most powerful healers do in Mexico, homemade herbal waters are cheaper in the long term and have the added benefit of bringing pure earth energies to your cleanse and your spiritual work.

In Mexico, washing yourself during *un baño* consists of pouring this herbal liquid from a gourd or other container, such as bottle, all over yourself from top to toe after you have soaped and rinsed yourself in the final stages of your bathing ritual. If you can access it, you may also use Santa Muerte soap. On sale in religious paraphernalia shops often known as botanicas in the US, it usually has a picture of Holy Death on it. Not everyone can afford a bathtub in Mexico, but if you have one, it is also appropriate to immerse yourself in a tub that contains tap water mixed with the elixir you have brewed. You can work with more specific herbs for more specific goals, which is why this technique is sometimes better than using *siete machos* and other premade mixtures, as you can tailor your ritual to your needs. As you select the herbs and boil the mixture, you can imbue the elixir with your positive intentions. These recipes are outlined here, for the practitioner eager to work with herbs.

A basic recipe for love, and to bathe a red statue that you are using to ask la Santa to bring love and sweetness into your home, is

* a generous tablespoon of rose petals, a stick of cinnamon, a tablespoon of rue, and a dash of honey in a medium-sized pot of water.

A general recipe for white or black statues whom you ask for protection, cleansing, and to protect yourself, is

* a generous tablespoon of sage, one of basil, and one of rue in a medium-sized pot of water.

A general recipe for a yellow or blue statue whom you are asking for success, scholastic or financial (and to bring this luck into your life), you can also bathe in:

* one generous tablespoon of laurel, one of basil, and one of rue in a medium-sized pot of water.

A general recipe for a purple statue whom you are asking for health and to create your herbal healing bath is

* a generous tablespoon of rosemary, one of rue, and one of lavender in a medium-sized pot of water. You can swap lavender for garlic also.

A general recipe for a gold statue, for financial success and abundance, is

* one generous tablespoon of laurel, one of rosemary, and one of chamomile in a medium-size pot of water.

Once you have bathed and your mixture is ready, pour some of it in a receptacle, such as a large bowl or goblet, on your altar. With a soft cloth, gently clean the statue. If her gown is made of fabric, simply wet her face and toes tenderly. Following this, light your candles to welcome Santa

Muerte. If in doubt as to which color candles to use, a multicolored *siete potencias* is always a good choice, as is a white votive, the most neutral of all colors. Light your incense at this point and drift the smoke plumes around the statue, and yourself, to cleanse both the statue and yourself. After this, stand your Santa Muerte statue in the bowl as you use another goblet to pour the herbal liquid over her skeleton. Again, if her gown is made of material, simply do this to her face and bony extremities. Then recite the following petition:

> *Santa Muerte, Most Holiest Death of my heart,*
> *I call upon you to come to this place*
> *And to take this image as your own,*
> *which I now bless*
> *in the name of the Father, of the Son, and of the Holy Spirit,*
> *Let it be so.*
> *Amen.*

If you are open to tobacco, you may use a cigar or cigarette to further purify your statue, blowing smoke over her in an act of *sahumacion* (sacred fumigation). You may also place a cigarette or cigar in her hand or other suitable location and let her puff on it. At this point, you may further choose to name your statue. You might prefer to wait before naming your statue to further discover the character of your effigy, and ask her to guide you as per which name she wishes to have. You will have to use your intuition to guide you in this matter.

In Mexico, devotees choose a wide variety of names for the folk saints; these could be common female names such as Rosa or Luisa, or more esoteric names like *Angel de las Sombras* (Angel of the Shadows), *la Guerrera* (the Warrior), or even inspired by pre-Hispanic death deities, like Mictecacihuatl. Either way, these are names that devotees have carefully selected or that la Santa has whispered to them in a dream. In all cases, monikers must be respectfully allotted and, once appointed, should not be changed unless you determine that the Powerful Lady is not happy with her appellation.

Cleansing Your Statue

Negative energies and even evil or demonic spirits can enter into your statues at any time, especially if they have had much ritual use or there has been much negativity around you. It is easy to tell if this has happened: if things keep going wrong for you or bad events happen around your shrine all the time or in your house, such as things falling, unnerving noises—especially at night—or numerous fights. For this reason, statues must be regularly cleansed. To do so, make the herbal potion and bathe them or clean them, then fumigate them with tobacco and/or incense on a regular basis, and say a prayer. As detailed in the introduction, if energies are good, you may feel that fumigating your statue is enough, but either way, keeping her free of dust is important. Maintaining a clean altar will keep evil at bay.

You should be aware that a statue may break, as may other holy items shatter on your altar. This is not a cause for immense concern but an omen that negative forces are at work against you, but you are protected by la Santísima Muerte. However, do not remain idle and ignore the event. Make sure you cleanse yourself and your altar when this happens. I have been told by many a devotee that when a statue breaks, it is Santa Muerte protecting you and taking on the negativity that was directed at you. It is important to pay attention to the circumstances in which she broke. If someone was being negative with you at that time or even roaming around your altar, then you can be sure that this person bore you ill will. Take measures to protect yourself, and call on the Powerful Lady to protect you with her scythe by cutting away evil around you or covering you with her mantle so that no evil enters your heart or home. Prayers in chapter six are useful for combatting such evil.

If a sacred item breaks in such a manner that you can easily put it back together, such as a statue split down the middle that can easily be fixed, repairing it is okay if that can be done with glue fairly easily. Having said that, be sure to cleanse the item thoroughly first and pray over it, using one of the prayers provided for protection, against envy, or against whatever you believe is fitting for that ill energy. Nevertheless, you should not attempt to repair a shattered statue; instead, you must bury it in a sacred, natural location, such as a yard or park, and give it a sweet farewell, a funeral of sorts, and honor its spirit, thanking Santa Muere for her protection.

Broken candles should never be used and must be discarded immediately. Whether they broke on their way home from the store, in a package mailed to you, or once on your altar, they are of no use as they have absorbed a negative force that cannot be undone, and if you attempted to use them in ritual, they would only bring bad luck. Because sacred items absorb the energies of others, especially if they bear you ill will, it is recommended that you do not share your altar with anyone unless you are sure that their intentions are pure. I have seen this with my own eyes and had statues shatter after a jealous visitor gazed upon them. I knew Santa Muerte was warning me of their ill intentions and absorbing the brunt of the cruel energy.

Likewise, do not allow anyone else, unless you trust them deeply, to carry your candles or other sacred items home from the store for you. Furthermore, do not let others touch the items on your altar unless you trust them, as they may infuse the items with jealousy or other negativity. If others do handle your sacred items and you are aware that they may have imbued the items with ill intentions, you must cleanse those items and pray over them before proceeding with any further spiritual work. All of this is why those who own large shrines in Mexico purify them, as I have seen, once weekly with smaller rituals, and carry out a large and significant monthly spiritual cleansing rite.

Moon-bathing Ritual

Moon-bathing your statues is an excellent means of cleansing them for those who have access to a private yard or balcony. The energy of the moon works double duty. Not only does it cleanse your statues, ridding them of all malevolent forces, but it also suffuses them with the celestial energy of the lunar planet, allowing your spells, prayers, rituals, and hexes to work rapidly and with intense power. Santa Muerte is deeply connected to the moon, which is her planet; thus, allowing her to connect to her astral home is key.

To moon-bathe your statues, simply place them outside during a full moon, ensuring they face the luminary fully so that they are entirely illuminated in lunar rays. If you have an ample outdoor space, it is also recommended that you do a full ritual with bathing, incense, and fumigation, just as the best shamans do in Mexico. Performing such a magical ritual beneath the full moon will ensure you have the highest of celestial blessings from la Santa, and you will feel the mystical power of the moon stream into you, as well as the other elements, such as wind flowing through you and her. Furthermore, you can freely pour herbal liquids onto your Santa statues without having to care for receptacles catching the overflow, and this will allow your movements to be more carefree and aligned with nature.

Ritual Dressing of la Santa

A final consideration for those who have sewing skills or are of a creative nature is that you may choose to dress your Santa Muerte statue. Some devotees dress la Santa in bridal wear for marriage petitions. Not every devotee does this, and speaking for myself, as someone simply hopeless at embroidery, I would never even attempt it. Nevertheless, some devotees have skills and are called upon spiritually to garb their statues in unique gowns. For the skilled devotee, this constitutes another way of bonding with your statue and is furthermore useful as you need have only one statue whom you dress according to the color of your petition: a red gown when petitioning for love, white for cleansing, gold for bringing abundance to you, and so on.

If you choose to dress your statues, you should follow what devotees do in Mexico. Every month, change the gown of your Santa during a ritual dedicated to this, which will also double up as a cleansing ritual. At this point, undress la Madrina, cleanse her with an herbal bath, fumigate her, place the new gown on her, and then pray to her. You may also make promises to her through her wardrobe offerings. For example, if you wish for her to come through on a petition of love, you can vow to make her an opulent evening gown of red, embroidered with gold with pink taffeta finishes, if she delivers on her promise. You may also pledge her a bridal dress should your boyfriend ask for your hand in marriage, or a golden gown if she delivers a money miracle.

If you do not like sewing but like to accessorize, you can adorn your Most Holy Death statue with accoutrements that, once again, can serve as offerings or as a thank you for a petition she came through on. In Mexico, these accessories are varied. For example, some devotees gift their statues wigs, and certain devotees offer their effigies stunning necklaces, spangly tiaras, regal crowns, embellished scarves, or even purses. Of course, the size and number of such items will depend on the size of your statue.

Times of Day and Night to Work with Santa Muerte

When commencing any ritual, prayer, spell, or hex, you must consider the time of day or night and, of course, the position of the moon. Santa Muerte is deeply intertwined with the power of the moon, from whence she derives her energy and mysteries. Therefore, the different moon phases must be taken into consideration, for they will imbue your spells and spiritual work with their unique properties. Most devotees prefer to work at night for potent *brujeria*, but the day serves well for prayers of all sorts, simple spell work, and benevolent work with white candles. Many devotees I have met also recommended the early morning hours for work to do with new beginnings, attraction of money, and business prosperity, believing that their spiritual act will set the tone for the day to come.

Hexes and banishing work that seek to repel and return evil energy to the sender must be undertaken under the cover of darkness, preferably after midnight. Love sorcery spells to control and dominate the object of your affections, making them filled with lust for you and only you, known as *dominios*, should also be done around midnight, as should any other sort of binding spells. For more nefarious work, the later the hour, the better. I was told by a *bruja* that the hours after midnight, when the stygian gloom is at its thickest, darkest, and most opaque, especially from two to four o'clock, are the strongest hours for working malevolent magic. In Mexico, this is when narcos, criminals, and other magic workers who supplicate the Powerful Lady for pernicious petitions, such as death to their enemies, are known to work.

Each lunar cycle is distinct and will offer distinctive benefits; thus, you must wisely select from these for optimal results. For example, the waning moon is an optimal time to do spells to remove negative energies such as envy or to repel gossip. The dark moon phase is ideal for darker *brujeria* and the most malevolent of magic, such as hexing and cursing. It is also an excellent time for necromancy, should you wish to call on the deceased and converse with them through Santa Muerte, as she serves as a conduit for the dead. A lunar eclipse, when the moon disappears entirely from the night sky, is the *ne plus ultra* moment to perform a heinous hex of the most abominable kind. Such eclipses are rare, so you must plan in advance. Second to an eclipse for performing a hideous hex is a moonless, starless night when the blackness is so intense and thick that you could cut it with a knife.

* The waning moon is a good time for more nefarious spell-work, when for example, you want to make someone shut up, or to dwindle their prosperity, for anything related to lessening things, for example, for someone to have less love or happiness in their life.

* The new moon is particularly potent for when you are doing spell or prayer work that has to do with new projects, are starting something from scratch, or wish to break a bad habit such as smoking or drinking.

* The waxing gibbous moon is an opportune time for drawing spells and *brujeria* to attract things you wish to increase, such as love, sex, good health, or money, or to make something grow, like a business venture or a baby.

* The full moon is the time when you can connect the most fully with la Santísima Muerte. This is when the moon is at her most fertile, overbrimming with intensity and pure energy. You can channel this and harness it for any spell work, and it is ideal for love magic and sex sorcery, benefitting from the shining power ball that is the moon to supercharge your work. Some devotees make full moon water for cleansing by placing a bowl of water under the light of the full moon to charge it.

Attributes of Santa Muerte and How to Work with Them

You will notice that statues of Santa Muerte have specific attributes, and you might wish to focus on them, as is done in Mexico, such as meditating on the item, wafting smoke of incense or tobacco over them, and otherwise honoring and tapping into their powers. You may also choose to ask Most Holy Death to use the item to help you in your prayer.

The Book of the Dead

The Book of the Dead is a large and heavy tome that some statues of Most Holy Death feature. In such statues Santa Muerte holds the sacred book with both hands; it contains incantations and magic formulae, symbolizing her knowledge of the secrets of life and death, and her wisdom of witchcraft, spells, and sorcery. Focusing on the Book of the Dead will enable you, as a devotee, to tap into the spiritual realm and its secrets. Lighting a purple candle and praying to the Lady of the Shadows to aid you to develop your supernatural vision and abilities while tapping into the Book of the Dead will aid you on your spiritual journey and can also enable you to talk to the spirits of those who have passed so that you too can tap into the power of death. I have seen a spirit fly out of a statue holding the Book of the Dead; it swirled around the *brujo* who owned the statue before returning to its pages. After the soul had dissolved into the tome, the witch whispered to me a message from my deceased grandmother that was so deeply personal and accurate that I knew it was she who had visited us, speaking to me through Holy Death.

The Celestial Sphere

The celestial sphere, which in Mexico is referred to in prayer and by devotees as *la esfera celeste*, features on some Santa Muerte statues instead of the typical globe, which I detail below. The sphere may be transparent, silver, white, or another translucid color. It often looks like a crystal ball or orbicular gazer. It has multiple meanings. On the one hand, *la esfera celeste* refers to heaven and the afterlife in many Mexican prayers to Santa

Muerte; thus, the celestial sphere symbolizes Santa Muerte's power as a psychopomp who takes us to the heavens where we will find peace, rest, and rejoin our dearly departed. As such, the sphere may be used to meditate on mortality or communicate with the dead. But also as a crystal ball, the sphere may be used to divine the future. You may gaze into it to receive messages from Santa Muerte and those in the heavens who will guide you through visions directly received in the gazer or through dreams and visions sent from the celestial realms.

The Globe

Santa Muerte holding the globe sends us the message that there is no place where she is not present. Death is everywhere. She does not distinguish between the beings of this earth. All the land is hers, as are all the people, animals, and plants—everything belongs to her. For her, there are no borders, no place she does not go, deep even in outerspace, beyond the globe and into the galaxies—all is hers.

The globe is a symbol of power, and being able to hold the world in your hands indicates that you have power in any area of life. If you're a devotee seeking success in any area, it is recommended you focus on this globe so as to ensure achievements, whether in business or academic endeavors or other ventures. Call on Most Holy Death to help you harness the power of her globe to give you confidence, leadership skills, and independence. Women and men who seek to empower themselves in their careers would be particularly advised to tap into the power of Death's globe. Also, for prayers concerning world peace or global healing, the globe is an ideal focal point. For example, during the COVID-19 pandemic, I have seen a *curandera* focus on the globe asking Holy Death to cleanse the earth of the virus and the poverty, misery, and troubles the pandemic context has caused.

The Holy Mantle or Sacred Cloak

Santa Muerte's sacred cloak flows around her bony form, covering it from head to bony toe. It symbolizes the unobstructed flow of energies essential for things to come into fruition, which she can cause to gush forth without obstacles for the faithful devotee, due to her powerful hold over life and death. It also signifies her ability to protect her secrets and mysteries beneath that mantle, as well as to safeguard the lives, homes, and businesses of devotees, shielding them from harm. Doña Queta once recounted that a group of aggressors was about to cross her path when she was walking home late at night. She was sure they would see her and mug her, but she prayed to la Madrina, and Santa Muerte covered her with her Holy Mantle so that they did not see her, and she walked home safely to her family. Such a story illustrates the power of the sacred cloak. Call on the Bone Mother to cover your home, family, loved ones, business, or yourself for protection. Visualize it covering anything you need to be protected so that it cannot be seen or reached by evil influences or enemies. The black cloak is the best to visualize when asking for her protection from enemies, but I recommend it be balanced by her white one, if possible, which will bring light and goodness, balancing the darkness of the blackness with its purity. You may wish to add her red robe too, if you want to protect those you care deeply for in a mantle of never-ending love.

The Hourglass

The iconic hourglass consistently refers to the passing of time and reminds us that our existence here on Earth is fleeting. But in Mexico, death is not about finality; it is about rebirth and renewal. I was told by a *curandero*: "We turn the clock over, and suddenly we start again. Death is not the End; it is only a necessary change in our lives where a new cycle begins."

The hourglass transmits several messages from Santa Muerte. First, she is telling us that death is not the end and that it is possible to speak to the spirits of those who have gone. Also, she is saying that when one door in our life closes, another will open. Things die to be reborn, so we must be patient as they grow. Also, Saint Death's hourglass tells us that we should not live at an accelerated pace, but live with patience, cherishing that which is important, and focus on the goals that are precious to us in this brief life upon Earth. Meditate upon the hourglass when you feel caught up in the rat race; it will help you prioritize what is truly important in life. You may also contemplate the hourglass when one chapter in your life is closing and a new one is opening.

The hourglass can help you to cope with things that take time. You may call on Santa Muerte to give you the fortitude to endure through difficulties and problems that take time to resolve. For example, the hourglass helped me recover from an illness I could not shake off for a while. After eating some contaminated food high in the beautiful mountains of the Sierra Madre del Sur, I was impatient to resume my travels but had to stay put. Through the hourglass, Santa Muerte teaches us patience. For example, one does not always heal overnight, and by contemplating the hourglass, one learns to be grateful for each day as blessings may take time, just as my stomach took time to heal, a time during which I learned the importance of perseverance. You can also place an hourglass on your shrine if you do not have access to a statue with one. Or, if you have no hourglass, a watch serves the same purpose, and I have used one to petition Santa Muerte to help me through a long, slow healing process.

The Lantern

The lantern is a symbol of Santa Muerte's intelligence and lucidity, representing her ability to bring light to situations. Focus on the lantern to bring clarity to the path you are on. The lantern also reminds us to step out of the darkness of ignorance and to seek transparency and light in our undertakings. The lantern with its warm, glowing light also signifies comfort, peace, and harmony, especially within the home, and can be used to bring this to places where they are lacking. Finally, the lantern reminds us to be a light to those who need us to bring clarity, peace, and beauty in their times of darkness. As a writer and artist, I have meditated upon the lantern, asking la Santa Muerte to help me bring light, knowledge, and wonder through my work to the world. You too may be inspired in whatever job or undertakings you have to call on the lantern to bring light where and when it is most needed.

The Owl

The owl in Mexico is associated not only with wisdom, as in European lore, but also with death. The old Mexican maxim "When the owl screeches, the Indian dies" reminds us of the importance of owls as omens of imminent death. If an owl visits you, as a devotee, it could be a message that someone close to you will die, but it could also be a reminder to look deeper into things.

The owl is a nocturnal bird that has infallible sight. At the side of Most Holy Death and as her messenger animal, it signifies the skeleton saint's ability to read deeply into the heart of all situations and invites you to seek deeper meanings too. The owl's huge eyes, which are able to see even on the darkest of cloudy nights, remind us not to be blinded by appearances and to consider things carefully. The owl, who represents wisdom, advises us to act wisely in life with all information available to us and with foresight. You may also call on the owl, who flies over danger, to help you evade danger, soar over troubles, and fly from troublesome people or places.

One of the owl's main functions is as messenger of Santa Muerte. For this reason, if you need insight into your problems, seek spiritual guidance, or wish for a murky situation to be clarified, you should focus on the owl who will bring counsel, illuminating the path on dark nights of the soul. The owl can also take your message to the Lady of the Shadows. By lighting purple, white, and black candles; burning mugwort as incense upon your altar; or drinking Aztec dream grass, mugwort, or valerian tea before sleep, you may call on Holy Death and her owl to fly to you in your dreams and to bring you the knowledge you require to make decisions and guide you in your activities. I have seen owls at the most powerful shrines in Santa Muerte, and one perched on my windowsill hooting the night before I learned of the blood pact to Santa Muerte for the first time. If you see one, it is a vital message from Santa Muerte. Do not ignore it. Honor its spirit.

The Scales of Justice

The scales are an ancient symbol of justice. They represent Santa Muerte's ability to mete out divine justice, and it should be noted that justice is whatever your own perspective is. In Mexican practice, there is no fixed notion of right or wrong. For there is an understanding that good and bad are in constant fluctuation and that what is right for one person could be wrong for another; indeed, what is wrong today could be right tomorrow and vice versa. I have even known members of the same family to pray to *la Madrina* for opposing prayers with an understanding that whoever was the more devoted to Death would be heeded! This lack of fixed notion of morality and shifting righteousness is why you can ask Santa Muerte for whatever you like, and she will never judge you for it, and she understands that justice is whatever you deem it to be.

Focusing on the scales of justice is excellent if you have to go to court or have legal issues; Santa Muerte will take your side no matter what you did, and she will aid you with matters related to law, authority, and disputes of all sorts. You may pray to the Powerful Lady for justice, lighting a green candle and following the prayer in chapter six, and you should focus on the scales, honoring her power to bring forth righteousness as you exhale tobacco smoke on them or waft incense above, below, and around the scales.

The scales are also associated with balance and equality, conveying the fairness that Santísima Muerte treats us with, for before death we are all equal. They also remind us of the importance of balance in life and her ability to bring that to us, especially inner peace in our being. The scales may help us find stability, security, and peace. If you have addiction problems or other bad habits—such as a tendency to overspend or keep bad company, or act out with loved ones—that cause your life to be out of balance, you can pray to Santa Muerte and ask her to help you find strength to overcome these behaviors. You can even waft extra incense around the scales or move them physically, either tipping them and then letting them come into balance or swapping the left for the right, as you visualize balance coming to your life.

In Mexico, many devotees are moved to practice free-form prayer, and when pleas are earnest, they will always be heard, so I am told. I have heard devotees improvise on the spot, so I will not transcribe a petition I heard for balance verbatim for privacy reasons. But as an example, you might say something along these lines:

Most miraculous and powerful Santa Muerte, I come before you humble and aware that my life is not in harmony through my own fault. Please, Santísima Muerte, use the power of your scales to teach me to find balance and give me the strength to create stability in my life to overcome (*add your petition for your personal problem here*).

·····✻·····

The Scythe

The scythe is Santa Muerte's lethal weapon and symbolizes the folk saint's absolute power to cut bad things away from our lives, whether it be ridding us of enemies, illness, bad habits, or other negativity, such as self-destructive energy or jealousy from others. You can call on the Powerful Lady to rid you of these things by focusing on her scythe and imagining her using it to slash away that which you want removed. For example, you can visualize her cutting cancer out of an ill body, or sweeping away a tornado, even whacking down an enemy or severing their mortal cord if you think they deserve it. Praying to her and asking that she wield that scythe to help you will further the act. Remember that if you are not respectful to the Powerful Lady and do not honor a promise to her, she may also use the scythe to thwap you on the head, or worse, as a reminder of her power and your place at her feet. When she comes through on a petition you have asked, you must always gift her something, be it a libation, flowers, food, or other offering.

The scythe is also a tool that has been for used for millennia to harvest crops. It symbolizes reaping what you sow and your ability to grow the seeds of good fortune, health, and happiness. You may also focus on the scythe as an instrument that draws to you money, riches, abundance, wellness, love, and much more.

Insect and Animal Omens

Within Mexico, insect and animal omens are important to those deeply devoted to death and indeed to spiritual practitioners who work with *brujeria* and the old ways. *Curanderos, brujos,* and those dedicated to Holy Death for decades have all told me it is vital to watch out for them. Outside of Mexico, people sometimes fail to watch for signs from nature; therefore, dear reader, to help you be more attuned with the natural world through which the spirits speak to us, after years of study, I have collected all these omens so that you too can tap into the secret messages. Should these animals or insects be in or around your altar, in the offerings, or be seen at the window, or met at the door after or during prayer, or even dreamt of following a ritual to Santa Muerte, you can use this guide to interpret what they portend. They may also appear as symbols in tobacco or incense smoke or as images on offerings, such as a spot shaped in their form on a banana gifted to la Santa. Aside from these omens, skulls, scythes, and images of Santa Muerte may appear around or on your altar, and they are clear signs of her presence at your side.

If a positive sign blesses you, such as a beautiful bird hovering around the window near your altar, be sure to honor the animal, and in so doing honor la Santa Muerte. For example, during a time of harsh and heavy rain, when life was difficult for me, I was living in a leaky, damp house in Sonora and worried my house would flood; I prayed to Santa Muerte for a sign she would protect me and better days would come. Shortly after my prayer, a hummingbird appeared just outside my window and stared in at me through the rain. I knew it was an omen from Holy Death of wondrous things to come and an end to my troubles, but I also knew that the bird might have difficulty staying dry and fed in the wet weather. I wanted to care for it as Santa Muerte cares for me. I set up a feeder filled with sugar water which I placed under the dry eaves of my home. The bird came every day to feed, and soon after, the rains stopped and better days of sunshine and beauty blessed me through Santa Muerte's bony hand.

* *Ants:* Envy, low-frequency energy, and witchcraft done against you, especially if red.

* *Bats:* Tap into your intuition, visions, and dreams.

* *Bedbugs:* Infidelities, marital problems, family poverty issues.

* *Bees:* Positive omens of tenderness and love; may also refer to constancy in work, employment, or business.

* *Beetles:* Health problems in older adults in the house or in your family.

* *Birds:* Feelings of lack of freedom, a desire to stretch your wings and fly.

* *Butterflies:* Good news, prosperity, and abundance; the support of spirits, especially loving family members or friends who have passed on.

* *Centipedes:* Be careful of danger and betrayal.

* *Cockroaches:* People problems, low-frequency energy, and possibly fatigue from people who drain you or annoy you; may also signify envy, witchcraft.

* *Crabs:* A positive sign that perseverance and nurturing will bear fruit; renewal and rebirth as the crab sheds its shell to be reborn.

* *Crickets:* Gossip, slander.

* *Doves:* Happiness, peace, and tranquility.

* *Dragonflies:* Healing, positive changes, pure energy, tapping into your inner child.

* *Flies:* Disagreements, arrival of family problems.

* *Hummingbirds:* The arrival of a new love in your life, love in your couple, good luck, abundance and beauty.

* *Ladybugs:* Good luck, change in destiny; have faith things will go in your favor.

* *Large lizards:* A close family member or friend will gossip to others about you.

* *Lice:* Bad thoughts, mostly from older female figures, such as a mother or mother-in-law.

* *Maggots:* Beware! Malevolent magic and bad energy being sent your way.

* *Mice:* Do not be wasteful; otherwise, you will have financial issues. Conversely, if you pay close attention to details and labor hard, there will be money.

* *Moths:* Find your inner light; listen to your inner voice and fly free.

* *Owls:* Santa Muerte is watching over you; Death is near (could be an omen of death or a positive change).

* *Rabbits:* Fertility and productivity.

* *Rats:* An invitation for self-reflection and to examine your life. Does something need to be handled or cleared from your life?

* *Scorpions:* Hurt caused to you by others; betrayals and treason, especially by people known to you; presence of enemies visible or invisible.

* *Small lizards:* Someone is interested in you for a sexual liaison. If close to the items of your partner, then someone is interested in them.

* *Snakes:* Bad advice; envy; ignore comments from others who are envious and focus on your own knowledge.

* *Spiders:* Wisdom, protection, and power; if a large, biting spider, beware of enemies.

* *Squirrels:* Good luck if you work hard on your projects.

CHAPTER FIVE

❀ 💀 ❀

Colors and Candles

Working with votive candles is vital within Santa Muerte spirituality. Some devotees say a candle represents the devotee; the wax, your body; the flame, your soul. Others say that a votive is your prayer manifest, burning with all the desire you have for it to be realized and entrusted to Holy Death to make true. The candle is your key to asking *la Niña* to come through on specific petitions; therefore, any prayer must be accompanied by the act of lighting a votive first, followed by the prayer itself, as you focus on the flame. Burning votives is also a way of thanking her, honoring her, and communicating with Most Holy Death. Candles should be lit not only when you are asking for something but also in gratitude for a petition answered by Santa Muerte or just in general devotion and respect for Santísima Muerte. As she loves nothing more than to be gifted flowers and have candles lit, I advise you do this regularly. As with any family member or loved one who would not only want you to be nice when you want something, you also should show reverence and care without ulterior motive to *la Madrina*, so that means lighting candles without asking for anything and giving gifts with no demands attached. The beautiful, powerful Queen of Death expects and deserves to be spoiled.

I often light candles in thanks to Santa Muerte, as is common in Mexico. At the end of a long and dangerous journey—for example, crossing narco-territories and driving on hazardous roads where speed limits are frequently ignored and the roads are full of snaking twists and turns—I light a votive to the Bone Mother upon my return to my house to thank her for getting me home safely. Devotees also light a candle after a dream of Santa Muerte to thank her for visiting them and to keep the channels of communication open, alight with energy, so to speak. All prayers are activated by lighting a votive candle, as is *brujeria*.

Specific candles are sold in Mexico for working with Most Holy Death. In the US, they can also be found in botanicas and Latino markets. Abroad, and in general outside Mexico, candles can also be obtained online, and even in Pagan shops or more conventional ones, such as Walmart.

In Mexico, the most commonly sold candles feature the oldest known image of Santa Muerte on them, with scales and globe, surrounded by skulls, usually with the words *Muerte contra mis enemigos* (death to my enemies) on the bottom of the glass jar. These candles do not have labels on them; the image is etched directly onto the glass. They come in all colors, in line with the color correspondences indicated later in the chapter. Such candles are popular in Mexico, including the original Santa Muerte votive. I recommend them if you can find them as they burn well, you can observe the wax easily as there is no label hiding it, and the votive has strong spiritual power given that it displays the first known image of Most Holy Death.

Candle selections have increased across Mexico, and indeed the world, and now you can find all sorts of differently decorated candles that have la Santa Muerte's image on them and that are equally worthy of her worship. Many candles now feature labels, which vary hugely in design and quality. Gel candles have become popular; they feature a hard wax figure of the skeleton saint within a soft, transparent gel around her form so that this is visible through the jar. Such candles are often charged with seeds and charms. Outside of Mexico, it is harder to find the traditional candles, and the markets are flooded with an array of different decorations and symbols of Saint Death. These often feature printed labels stuck to candles by online entrepreneurs. Moreover, cognizant that some devotees are English-speaking, many votives now have English wording and even prayers on them, referring to Santa Muerte as Holy Death, and in one instance I even saw her dubbed St. Deep Death!

I recommend candles that have a clear depiction of Santa Muerte on them. If you can get those of Mexican origin, all the better. Votives sold with large, thick labels tend to be difficult to watch as the flame is hidden by the label. It is important to watch the flame, as you will learn. Such thick-labeled candles often burn badly because the label prevents the flow of oxygen, causing the flame to go out. Another important factor is the quality of the wax. As you will find, some brands of candles burn better than others, so stick to those that burn well and do not pool with weepy wax. Also, it is clear that some candles appear to have more spiritual potency or are better received by the skeleton saint. I have been told that she will express her happiness when she likes a candle, and certainly, I have seen her grin when I have lit one of her favorites. Above all, the right color, as I describe in this chapter, is the most important thing.

Candles are the cornerstone of devotion, and even if you cannot get a Santa Muerte votive, a generic candle will do to commence your devotion or to thank the Bone Mother, especially in a pinch. A generic candle is better than none at all. In Mexico, I have met devotees who could not even afford a statue but only a generic candle for their altar. But with a small offering, they told me, this sufficed to make their prayer and did not prevent the skeleton saint from making good on their plea, for they had faith and devotion to Most Holy Death. For the thrifty neophyte, be aware that Santa Muerte will not judge you should you start with but a small altar or but a plain candle. Everything has to start somewhere, and unlike in other faiths where financial investment is sometimes equated with spiritual return, the Powerful Lady does not judge the devotee who has little in their pocket as long as they have much faith in their heart.

Activating Your Altar

Any Santa Muerte altar must, when active, feature burning candles. Fire is a powerful, essential, and elemental energy. It can destroy, but it can also create. Most of Santa Muerte *brujeria* hinges on this double-edged ability to destroy what is bad and to create what is good for you in your life. The flame also communicates and makes palpable those hopes, dreams, and desires you carry in your heart. As I was told by a witch in Acapulco, "The burning flame is a bridge between the natural and the supernatural world and will convey your petitions at the elemental level. The flame can also give you access to extrasensory powers and perceptions. The flickering lit wick can tell you secrets and make dreams into reality." Fire is thus an essential element in your shrine. As detailed in chapter three, the altar must have four elements—water, air, earth, and fire—to which is often added a fifth essential element—faith. Fire and faith are critical ingredients requisite for any prayer to succeed.

Not everyone understands the secrets of candle work, and I learned only by watching and listening closely to the silver-haired witch of unknown years who would be my guide in the most occult aspects of my Santa Muerte research. A lit votive candle works by transmuting elements essential to nature into new forms: the solid form (wax) metamorphoses into air, fire, and water. In this way, as the witch explained: "The candle is a receptacle for prayer, containing your faith, hopes, and desires. It will transmit wishes, petitions, and dreams, releasing these requests into the world at a supernatural and immaterial level. Once it is lit, these essential energies evaporate and are freed through these elements into the world around us. From a spiritual plane, they then become transformed into tangible outcomes, items, and relations."

The energy from your mind nourishes the flame; thus, it is vital to focus on the fire, imbuing it with your intentions when you light a candle and pray over it, as well as later contemplate it as you humbly request Santa Muerte to heed your petition. Visualize your dreams becoming reality and let your aspirations fuel the flickering flame; imagine it growing and your petition transformed into reality. If you have a question, focus on the flame to enter into the cosmic realm and to learn the answer. Most Holy Death will answer if she deems your petition worthy or your question of relevance.

Technique

For prayers with candles to work, it is vital that you are able to focus on what you are asking. Unless you are engaging in malevolent magic, you should first be free of negative energy. Ensure your heart, soul, and mind are in the right place before lighting a candle. Wafting incense and/or tobacco over yourself, your altar, and even the candle is always advised. Then you use your hand and matches or a flaming incense stick to light candles. Never use a lighter or other mechanical igniter. Your hand, together with the earth energy of wood, must give birth to the candle flame, or the petition will not be heard. Wood, as I have already described, is an essential and spiritual material in Santa Muerte devotion. A *curandera* explained to me that wood's energy is sacred and hails from the earth. This allows it to transmit energies at a fundamental level, and the combination of earth (the match), fire (the flame), and your hand (faith) is an important trifecta for supplications to be seeded in the supernatural cosmos and to create tangible outcomes in the real world.

It is for this same reason that wooden relics and death art, whether statues, skulls, or carvings of owls, are often visible on altars and in shrines across Mexico. Earth energy is necessary on an altar as it grounds your work and you, bringing outcomes in the earthly realm. It balances water, which is ethereal, and although necessary to allow the flow of energies, will not absorb and then ground that energy as wood can. It also juxtaposes the volatility of fire and air, as wood, like stone, which is also excellent on the altar, is stable and solid. For this reason, candles should not be lit with anything but matches or burning incense.

Another rule of thumb is one candle for one petition. You must burn the candle all the way to the end, or the petition will not be heard. Outside of Mexico, I have seen people using the same candle for different petitions and blowing it out in between. This does not work. I repeat: *Only one petition per candle.* Also, one candle per person. If, for example, a family are all in danger, whether due to a contagious illness, violence, or a wild fire, you must light one candle per person. One candle will not suffice, as each flame represents one soul.

Prior to lighting a candle, rub it all over your body so it can absorb your energy, unless you are hexing someone or lighting the candle for someone else. If you are lighting the candle for someone else's health, if you can, rub it all over their body, from top to toe. The next step is to carve into the wax the initials of the person the prayer concerns, or if it is yourself, your own name. Use a sharp stick or other implement to etch these in the wax. In Mexico City, I have also seen more affluent devotees use an indelible marker to write the name of the person on the side of the candle. You can also print a picture of the person the prayer concerns and place it below the candle for extra efficacy.

If you are wishing for something concrete, like a car, it is useful to place an image of the car or even a toy car by the candle. For this reason, in Mexico, chapels often have many photos, images of items, and toys in them. You may also choose to write a letter to Santa Muerte, as is done across Latin America, asking humbly for her help. Express your needs, your devotion, and your understanding that this petition is in her power only. Also, promise to be a loyal devotee and to thank her should she come through. Then fold the piece of paper and place it by the candle as it burns. Hide it in your box when you are not there if you fear prying eyes. This is also a good place to keep the written prayer until it is fulfilled. This petition can also be put in Santa Muerte's hand. If she has a scythe in it, you can remove the scythe temporarily and roll up the prayer and place it in her hand, leaving it there until she comes through. At this point, replace the scythe and gift her generously.

Once your candle is lit and you have recited your prayers, keep it aflame all day and night long until it burns down to the base and no more wax is left; then discard the empty vessel. If the flame dies by itself, waft incense and/or tobacco over it and yourself, in a brief cleansing, and relight it once more. If the flame goes out again, this means this petition will not be heard and you must cleanse yourself thoroughly with an herbal cleansing bath (see chapter three) and incense/tobacco. Also, cleanse the candle by wiping it down with the herbal concoction; then relight it again. If the candle still fails to stay lit after this, you must first cleanse yourself and your altar as well as your statues. Take some time to reflect if anyone or anything is blocking you, and then work on releasing this through further cleansings, if necessary, and prayer. Only then should you purchase a new candle and start afresh with both prayer and votive.

It is not forbidden to remove excess wax from candles by pouring it out, or carving free the wick, and I have seen this done in Mexico when votive wax is drowning the flame. Gel candles are sometimes fickle, and may require more care than the traditional candles that use pure paraffin wax. In Mexico, the gel candles are the most expensive, and many devotees cannot afford them; thus, traditional candles are more widely used.

However, I have found pure wax votives more reliable, despite the fact that it is easy to be drawn to the beauty of gel candles, which, if of good quality, burn fast and clean. If you find a brand that works for you, stick to it.

Note the moon phases before you light a candle. Align the moon's power as best as possible with your petition. If in doubt, a full moon is always an excellent time to start burning a votive. A nine-day prayer, known as a novena, in which you repeatedly pray for nine days in a row, is also highly recommended. Some devotees even choose to extend this to a month. You should also note that you may need to light more than one candle. In Mexico, I have seen devotees light the same color candle again and again, going through numerous votives, and saying the same prayer until their petition is heard.

This brief anecdote illustrates the benefits of lighting consecutive candles: My friend's child was sick with an undiagnosed illness. She and her mother lit a candle to la Santa Muerte, a white one of healing and purity, and then prayed a novena. The candle was burnt through by the end of nine days of prayer, but the child was still sick. The malady remained undiagnosed despite visits to doctors and blood tests. The family lit another white votive candle and once again said a novena, but the child still did not get better. Finally, they consulted a *curandero* and lit a third and final white votive candle; the healer also recommended herbal teas and more prayers. At the end of the last night of prayer and candle burning, the child recovered.

Word of Warning

Although many pure wax candles molded in the Reaper form of Death herself—or even skulls in the US—without a glass jar around the wax figure are now available online, I have seldom seen them used in Mexico on altars and at shrines, although they may be used in specific *brujeria*. I have no doubt this is due to the probability that should they topple over, a fire would surely start. I recommend you avoid these as most Mexicans do, above all because in terms of safety, the candles in glass jars are more secure and can be left burning all night with far less fear of fires starting than with the naked ones. It is only in *brujeria* that tapered candles, without glass jars, are burnt and useful as things can be etched all along the long body of the candle. They are also cheaper, so when many candles are needed, they are an economical option. Due to fire hazards, I recommend always placing a plate or other small, nonflammable item below the candle when burning it unattended, especially overnight, in particular if the surface upon which you placed it is combustible.

Nevertheless, fires are frequently caused by votives falling over or getting too hot and setting ablaze the surface they are on. In the local press, I see stories of conflagrations on a regular basis. A huge inferno once burnt down much of a famous Santa Muerte chapel in Sinaloa, incinerating most of its contents in 2011. Albeit in Santa Ana, El Salvador, when a huge fire destroyed the market, the only thing that survived was a figure of Santa Muerte, which was found "intact" amidst the rubble. Any statue that survives a blaze must be considered sacred, and devotees whose houses have burnt down with only an effigy of la Santa surviving know that such effigies have intense powers and should be turned to in deep devotion and never discarded even if they are sooty to the touch.

As you will note, once you start working with votives, the base of the glass candle jar can get extremely hot, especially when the wax burns out at the end, and the flame is close to the bottom. For this same reason, when your candle is in its last stages, with low wax levels, let it burn out. Do not attempt to put it out and relight it another day. As I have found, lighting a votive that has little wax left in it is hard. Given the wick is so far down in the jar, there is little oxygen to fuel the flame when lighting the wick, so you will have to hold a long, burning match or incense stick to the wick for a lengthy time. You can scald your hand in the process while clutching the glass jar, which will get hot quickly once a naked flame is within its walls.

Ideally, you should never put out a candle once lit for magical intent, but if you are understandably afraid of fire hazards and only want the candle burning under your waking attendance, then put out the flame when you leave your house or when you go to sleep, but remember to light it up as soon as you next can. When you extinguish the flame, never blow it out. You will blow all the energy away, and your petition will fail. Do not snuff it out because you are disrespectfully depriving the flame of oxygen and thus ridding your spell of energy. Use a spoon or other object to push the wick into the wax and then back out again, or shake the candle around till the wax hits the flame and extinguishes it. This way, the energy goes back into the candle itself, not dissipating into the air.

Combinations

You may wish to combine colors of candles. In Mexico, due to funds and facility, devotees generally light just one candle, but sometimes when the situation is serious, they may choose to mix and match various candles, usually in a duo or trio, to heighten the energy and make the spiritual work more specific to their needs. I have even seen a devotee light five candles that correlated to her needs. I advise the use of combined candles to the person who has a detailed and determined petition to make. Indeed, I was advised to do this by a *bruja* and have found it effective to mix and match, when I have felt that the *siete potencias* did not feel powerful enough for what I was asking and needed things to align.

The *siete potencias* candle is still most useful. You may incorporate a *siete potencias* with two other candles to empower them and align events, such as a witch once did for a client I knew who needed her husband to stop drinking. The witch lit an amber candle, against addiction, a white candle to purify and cleanse his body, and a *siete potencias* so that everything might line up and he see the need to stop drinking and regain a healthy life to support his family better. You will need to consult the color chart later in this chapter and decide how best to select and combine your colors. This is also advisable as prayers often require not only a petition for something but also a protection that something else will not happen. For this reason, devotees often add a white and/or black candle to any petition.

Another example of color combination follows: a devotee who was a close friend of mine feared that her son would be sentenced to a lengthy prison sentence after he was caught by the police with his friends taking part in activities I will not detail here for privacy reasons, but which you can guess.

She was not only scared her son would get a lengthy jail sentence but also that one of his friends would give him up and supply secret information to the police in exchange for a shorter sentence or none at all. She lit the green candle of justice so that he would not be sentenced, or if so, receive a light sentence. She lit a white candle for harmony and to bring light and positive energy to the situation. She also lit the candle known as *tapa boca* (shut your mouth; which I detail on page 119) to prevent anyone in her son's circle from squealing.

Colors of Candles

As detailed in the section "Colors of Statues" in chapter four, color symbology is vital in Holy Death spirituality. For your prayers to be heard, the color of the candle must be correct as it serves as part of your supplication to Santa Muerte. Choose the color based on the needs you have. Many devotees in Mexico only use Santa Muerte candles; however, sometimes resources are scarce, and they cannot be obtained. As I stated, at altars and shrines across the country, I have seen devotees use plain candles—often just white but sometimes of other colors too—contained within a glass jar. If you are in desperate need, this is not an issue. What is more important is devotion, faith, and focus on the flame. The colors were already introduced in the section in chapter four, but I will give greater details here so that you can prepare more thoroughly.

Amber

Amber is frequently used for petitions to Santa Muerte by those who have addictions and need her help to overcome their bad habits, or those who want to help heal people they know who have such issues—whether it is overcoming minor addictions such as an inability to stop eating junk food, spending money you do not have, or smoking cigarettes/vaping, or whether it is more serious vices such as gambling, alcoholism, drug addiction, and so on. In Mexico, this candle is found in rehab centers and also on personal altars. Often, worried family members will unite and pray to Santa Muerte over this candle, or a girlfriend, boyfriend, father, mother, wife, or husband may pray alone for their child or spouse. It is important, if you need Santa's help, to place a piece of paper by the votive with the full name of the addict, their date of birth, and if possible, a picture of them.

If you are addicted to something, Santa Muerte will not judge you, and will help you. In Mexico, addicts often make pacts with the Bone Mother, promising to honor her by not smoking weed or not drinking, for example, for a month or more. You should write out this promise on a piece of paper that features the date of the day you stopped smoking, drinking, taking drugs, or gambling and also features a date until which you promise to be clean by; you should then sign the document. In so doing, you acknowledge that if you break your promise to Most Holy Death, she will strike you down with her scythe and punish you as she sees fit. Excellent offerings include orange foods, flowers, and fruits, like tangerines, cantaloupe, bird of paradise blooms, and candy. You may wish to avoid gifting alcohol or tobacco if you need to dispense with addictions to these. Yet, conversely, you may choose to give these gifts to Holy Death, as is done in Mexico, with the understanding that they are hers and you cannot touch them, and if you do, she will punish you severely. As a *curandera* from Tabasco once told me: "Sometimes we give bad things to Santa Muerte, like lots of sugary candy, alcohol, and tobacco because we should not have them, but given to her, she will take them so we do not, and transform them into positive energy for us."

Black

Black is Santa Muerte's most powerful color. She may help you to gain force and influence with her black effigy and candle, and cause harm to your enemies or those who deserve to be punished for their actions. Black also proffers her protection from evil and harm, including the coronavirus, as well as from evil spirits, jealousy, and envy of others, although the reversible candle is an excellent choice for those too. You can light a black candle to petition her to remove curses or to exorcise demonic spirits from yourself or your altar, in which case I recommend a white candle too. This way, you bring in light at the same time.

A black votive can also be lit for purposes of *dark brujeria* to call on Santa Muerte to bring vengeance, danger, or even death to your enemies. This is the candle par excellence for hexes and curses. This candle brings forth Saint Death's powers as *la Niña Negra* (the Black Girl), who will reap destruction for you and sow discord. Couple a black candle with a statue of *la Niña Negra* to tune into through prayer and spellwork for maximum deadly potency. For warding off coronavirus, or any other evil energy that is causing you or your loved ones harm, light a black candle before your *la Niña Negra* and pray for her protection.

When hexing someone, you should always engrave their initials or full name, along with their date of birth (if you know it), in the candle wax before lighting it. You can also print a photo of them and place it by the candle. You may choose to mark out their eyes. You should also write a letter to la Santa expressing what you wish to befall the person. You should tell Santa Muerte of their crimes, exalting her name to give them the revenge they deserve. Focus all your evil intent on the candle prior to lighting it, and then once it's lit, let the flame burn with your hatred. Imagine it destroying them and everything they love through Santa Muerte's deadly power. Ideal offerings in this context are hard and dark liquor, such as rum and dark (*añejo*) tequila, as well as strong tobacco and darker-hued flowers. I like to give *la Niña Negra* smoky, aged mezcal (*reposado* and *añejo*), which she delights in.

My particular favorite is aged mezcal *con gusano*, which has a worm in the bottle. There are myths and legends in Mexico that the worm brings special powers. A good technique is to pour out a tall glass of mezcal replete with the worm in it and gift it to Santa Muerte. Then pour one for yourself without a worm in it. Following this, light a black candle to her. At this point, I usually drink a toast to Santa Muerte's sacred and dark potency; then I petition her to destroy my enemy and promise her gifts. After this, you can then visualize her placing the maggot inside your enemy with her scythe. Then imagine in your mind's eye the maggot slowly eating away inside your enemy's body, or nibbling away at their brain or soul, slowly destroying their life, home, or business from the inside out. *La Niña Negra* is also known (perhaps over and above, although all Saint Death's aspects will accept it) to enjoy marijuana, and will be happy to get high with you. Place some buds at her feet or light a joint and smoke it with her, giving her blowbacks or blowing smoke over her. Some devotees give her other drugs, too.

Black candles are rarely left in public chapels in Mexico. People prefer to burn them in the secrecy of their own homes, but I have seen several and once found a letter and a photo alongside it. I know the shrine owner well, and as she understood that I was researching hexes for the purposes of writing this book, she let me read the letter. Addressed humbly to Santa Muerte, it was from a jilted person who wished all the worst on their ex; they detailed a long list of atrocious events they wanted to befall that person, which I will not reveal for privacy reasons, but which will inform you of how detailed you can be in your imprecations. I asked the shrine owner about the letter, and she told me she knew the author who had been cruelly mistreated by their other half. The wise woman told me that people hurt and humiliated in love are heard by Santa Muerte.

As I stated earlier, *la Niña*, it is often recounted, was jilted at the altar on her wedding day and has no patience for men or women who mistreat their lover, fiancé/fiancée, or spouse. Rather than lighting a red candle to bring your beloved back, it may be that you are sick of trying to make things work with them and only want them out of your life and to suffer for all they have done to you. Santa Muerte will help you take revenge. If you're in love and someone who claims to love you back has, through their actions, shown they do not care about you, your feelings, or needs, or cheated on you with someone else, call on *la Niña Negra*. Likewise if a friend, family member, or business partner betrayed you, or if someone hurt you or your loved ones, stole from you, or swindled you. Speak to her, write her a letter, give her an offering, and ask her to take your side. Light a candle to her, pray to her, and tell her to darken their path and reap revenge on them for hurting you and/or your loved ones. Tell *la Niña Negra* to strike them down with her mighty scythe.

Blue

A blue candle calls on Santa Muerte to bring you wisdom, focus, understanding, powers of explanation, communication, and creativity, as well as allowing for accrued concentration. It is best paired with a statue of Holy Death in her azure gown, but as it may be beyond one's budget to buy every colored statue, a blue candle alone to any Santa Muerte statue will suffice. As I write these very words, upon my desk sits serene Santa Muerte *Azul*, as she is known in Spanish. She has given me focus, inspiration, support, and care. She has helped me tap into her power so that I may be a conduit for her spirit, and convey all you need to know within this book. When I cannot concentrate, I pray to her blue form and light a blue candle, asking her to calm my mind and give me insights, focus, and clarity. Students, academics, writers, artists, musicians, composers, architects, photographers, designers, public speakers, even politicians, and others whose jobs demand high concentration and creativity light this candle to increase intelligence, inspiration, and communication, and allow them to focus on their projects.

The blue candle is excellent to light when you need to pass any test, whether it be a driving test or other type of exam. It is a good choice prior to public speaking as you can call on Santa Muerte to allow you to speak with clarity and focus. Blue can increase patience and can also be used to improve business partnerships and friendships. Santa Muerte *Azul* aids with communication in any scenario where articulation and explanation are important. Blue Most Holy Death candles aid to resolve labor matters, whether to solve problems at work or to ensure your professional career unfolds successfully. Along with a green candle and a gold candle, this combination is excellent if you need to take legal action for workplace injuries. Gold and blue are the duo that will bring financial success to any business that depends on good relationships with others, wisdom, and insight. Blue items are excellent offerings, such as berries, blue corn, blue tortilla chips, Mexican Morning Glory, floss flower (also known as Mexican paintbrush flower), and other azure-colored items. You can also burn blue sage incense.

Gold

The gold candle is one of the most popular candles in Mexico and beyond. This candle of abundance is often known as *Muerte Oro* (Gold Death) and serves to call on Santa Muerte to bring you financial success, infusing your business with positive energy. Related candles that have the same function may also be purchased under the name of *ven dinero* (come to me, money), or *lluvia de dinero* (let it rain money) candle. For any financial prayers, burn the golden candle to request *la Niña Dorada* to bless you, your family, and your undertakings with prosperity. If you own a store, you can even discreetly burn a candle at the back of it, unseen by your clients, to draw them in and get them to spend money. If you have no such secret place, or your store is online, burn one on your altar. I have seen gold candles burning even in offices of lawyers who wanted to win big money in cases. I have also heard of people burning them prior to making a business transaction that had a high risk but high reward status.

The gold candle pairs well with the yellow, white, and even black candles if you are undertaking dangerous business deals where you need Santa Muerte's protection from an unreliable partner. The golden statue in duo with the gold candle is ideal for calling on all of *la Niña Dorada's* powers. Excellent offerings to gift when asking for financial success and prosperity are yellow flowers, fruits (like bananas and mangoes but, again, not sour fruits like lemon; otherwise, business may become bitter), vegetables (such as yellow corn), golden buns of bread, and libations (such as golden tequila or blond beer). When you're in serious need of money, I advise lighting the gold candle paired with the prayer known as *Ven Dinero* (or Come to Me, Money) during a nine-day period, tell Santa Muerte of your financial needs, and if you are true in your devotion, she may provide a miracle of money.

Green

The green candle in Mexico is hugely popular because miscarriage of justice is frequent there, as are lengthy incarcerations for minor crimes. But as the devotee will know, legal matters affect us all, no matter where we live. The green candle is thus essential, as with it, Santa Muerte will intervene on your behalf in all legal matters and bureaucratic issues, whether or not you were on the right or the wrong side of the law. The Bone Mother is not moralistic; she will take your side no matter the issue, regardless of definitions of good and bad, as long as you are good to her. She knows you may have done wrong out of desperation or simply because that is your lifestyle. She does not judge. She will help you out no matter what you did.

Of course, she is also particularly attentive to miscarriages of justice or to helping those who have been wrongly accused, framed, or sentenced to a term too long in respect to a minor crime.

The Powerful Lady will help you with any legal issue. As a mother, she will intervene to help you get custody of your children in a divorce case. She will also help you get your green card, help you be freed from jail, or get compensated for workplace injuries, or otherwise win any important court case. She can help if you are accused of traffic violations, to get you off lightly. Once, I was hurtling down a highway, in a hurry to reach my destination before dark, as I feared dangers that haunted those parts. I was caught well over the speed limit by a police offer and handed a hefty speeding ticket, but I appealed the fine and prayed that Santa Muerte might help me as I could not afford so much money. La Niña Verde turned the ear of a judge in my favor. He halved the sum demanded after listening to my side of the story and my fears of traveling alone across one of the most perilous highways in the region.

Santa Muerte will be your lawyer, advocating for you in all legal battles, but also administrative issues. This could also include problems at work where someone is accusing you of something, or where you are being unfairly treated by a mean boss or jealous rival. Call on Saint Death for justice so that your side of the story will be heard and recognized. If you need extra protection from someone trying to sully your name and get you in trouble, add a black candle so that Santa Muerte may shield you from their bad energy and a white candle to bring her light to your side. You could also swap white with yellow for success or a *tapa boca* to get them to shut up, or what is known in Mexico as the *ciega, sorda y muda*, a candle that will numb all your enemy's senses. Some devotees also use the trio of white, green, and gold, as the last candle is for the winning of money and will ensure the Powerful Lady helps to get you the cash settlement you are owed in a court case.

The green candle should be used in combination with the prayer for justice listed in chapter six. You can, for optimal results, pair it with a statue that is carrying the scales of justice. *La Niña Verde* is the best choice, but *la Niña Blanca, las Siete Potencias*, and *la Niña Negra* are also all good choices, the latter especially if the charges against you are severe. *La Niña Dorada* is a good choice if you need her assistance to get financial damages. Light the green candle prior to any court case to get the law on your side through the holy power of Santa Muerte. Excellent offerings for such petitions are green items, like green apples, avocados, also fresh basil and garlic, as potent protective earth items are ideal.

Pink

The red candle is most commonly used for love, but in recent years, the pink ones have surfaced for the purposes of creating long-lasting love, tenderness, and increasing amorous depth and loving compassion in relationships over and above passion, domination, lust, or obsession, which are more associated with the red candle. Pink candles bless you with Santa Muerte's gentle loving energy creating a union based on mutual understanding and deep connection. When you want your relationship to be based on more than carnal desires, and want sweetness, softness, or sympathy from your spouse or lover, light the pink candle and call on *Santa Muerte Rosa*. Give her gifts of pink colors, such as pink roses, guava, ruby grapes, apples that have a pink hue to them, and burn rose incense. Honey, chocolates, and cinnamon for sweetness and a bit of spice are always well received.

Purple

In her purple potency, Santa Muerte governs powers of physical and supernatural healing. The purple candle calls on *la Madrina* to help you remove sickness, whether caused by natural or supernatural causes. When concerned about the health of a loved one, I often turn to purple Santa Muerte together with her pure sister, white Santa Muerte. The mauve candle also empowers *brujeria*, giving the devotee access to spiritual realms and occult guidance from Santa Muerte. In her purple cloak, the Lady of the Shadows is a gatekeeper between this realm and the astral, supernatural realms; thus, a purple candle alongside a violet statue allows you to connect deeply to the celestial worlds through Death's bony hand, and for this reason it is popular on the altars of powerful witches across Mexico. Indeed, it was Santa Muerte in her purple cloak who appeared to me in my dreams whispering in her deathly tones to share her mysteries and write this book that you now peruse, dear reader.

I have most often seen her across Mexico in the presence of witches. At Catemaco market, in Veracruz—among the most famous witchcraft markets in all of Mexico—I met a *bruja* dispensing spiritual advice and offering spell work from a bazaar stall adorned with a purple statue alongside a mauve candle, which she claimed was the most powerful for divination and activation of enchantments. She also had a black candle and a white candle burning on either side, which, she told me, reflected her ability to dispense both blessings and curses.

You can light a mauve candle to Santa Muerte alone or combined with other candles to work spells and obtain from her deep understandings of *brujeria*. The purple candle transforms energies from the cosmos, allowing you to transition from negative to positive states. If you feel there are energetic blockages in your life, light this candle. Since the color purple in Santa Muerte magic is associated with the psychic realm and accessing other dimensions, you can work with this votive to divine the future, increase psychic abilities, obtain prophetic dreams from her, and find spiritual peace and harmony. Whether asking Santa Muerte for help with *brujeria*, divining the future, or healing a physical sickness, mauve offerings are ideal. Lavender in both oil and flower form, eggplants, purple blooms such as irises, Mexican petunias, and other violet items should be placed on the altar. To empower benevolent magic, add an ivory candle to your mauve; to add extra power to malevolent magic, add the ebony votive to the violet.

Red

Red is used to tap into Santa Muerte's powers pertaining to love, romance, passion, sex, and desire. A red candle is lit to attract a new lover or keep your loved one faithful and attentive. Additionally, it can also be burnt for well-being and harmony within your couple. Bond with your *Niña Roja* statue and light many crimson candles for amorous and sexual petitions. Red also inheres domination and being in control in a relationship, so you can light a red candle to ask Santa Muerte to dominate someone in love and/or the bedroom so that they lust after you and only you, and are your submissive, sexual plaything. Placing their sex-soiled undergarments by the candle of love and reciting one of the relevant spells or prayers from this book may ensure their sexual fidelity, if you have Santa Muerte's power on your side. The first known prayer to Santa Muerte was for women who called on Holy Death for love sorcery to return a wayward lover/spouse who had strayed. It petitioned Most Holy Death to bring him back humbled and submissive at the woman's feet. The Powerful Lady is attentive to the prayers of those hurt in love. Therefore, if you feel your loved one is lacking in attention for you, or think they might be unfaithful or distracted by things other than you, light a red candle and recite the oldest known prayer to *la Niña Roja* to return a wayward lover, as detailed in chapter six.

Red roses, red apples, chocolate or candy, sugar, honey, and cinnamon are excellent offerings to *la Niña Roja* for love spells and prayers. Sweet things and the gifts of lovers should all be given as a thank you when your petition is answered. Never place any sour fruits, salt, or other such items on your altar, or you will bring that bitterness into your love life. This includes, for example, never placing green apples or limes during a love petition. Items must be warm, saccharine, and can have aphrodisiac powers, such as cinnamon or ginger candy. Alcohol is always appreciated. Tequila and mezcal are typical, but I have seen Irish cream liquor, beer, and even whiskey on altars. Although red wine is not typical in Mexico as it is expensive and reserved for the upper classes, I have seen some devotees offer it to *la Niña Roja*, and it is acceptable.

For the ultimate love petition, carve the initials of your beloved into the wax, with their date of birth, and print out a photo of them or a photo of the two of you together, and place it by your candle. You may add an object that belongs to them, such as a worn piece of clothing or jewelry—anything that is imbued with their essence. A letter can also be added, detailing your petition, which you may read to la Santa Muerte before you fold it up and place it by the red candle or tuck it into your Holy Death's hand or behind her globe. As you watch the flame burn and grow, visualize the passion your beloved has for you growing stronger, warmer, and hotter, like the flickering fire. Bottom line: in any love petition, you can use red.

Silver

Silver candles and statues are among the hardest to come by but are useful because they bring luck, lunar energy, money, and stability. In rituals to Santa Muerte, some people light silver, gray, or copper candles because they disrupt any negative energy that is in the way. Silver Santa Muerte candles help us to unblock all problems related to finances and the economy, as well as to conclude and close all pending business. Silver has long been mined in Mexico, far before the colonial era when the Spanish colonizers made huge profits off the extensive supply. It is thus associated with riches and financial well-being for some devotees. Other followers of Holy Death have informed me that silver allows the devotee to connect with the power of the moon, and in combination with purple and white or black votives, it can be powerful for working *brujeria* where *la Madrina's* lunar energy is required to augment potency. Ideal gifts when working with silver are silver-colored and diaphanous items, whether these are jewels, gem stones, or other such sparkling items, as well as generous offerings of water in crystal glasses and unaged silver mezcal (also known as *joven*).

White

When you need Santa Muerte's power of purity, cleansing, or positivity in general, this is the candle to use. White is also an excellent choice in petitions for health. This color brings forth harmony—physically, mentally, and emotionally—and when used in combination with *la Niña Blanca* will make any heavy situation seem lighter. *La Niña Blanca* alleviates, heals, and harmonizes. Lighting a white candle to her helps to purify the environment and calls on Santa Muerte to protect us from negative energies. She brings well-being, relaxation, and personal calm.

In Mexico, the white candle is one of the most ubiquitous in shrines and altars, as it can improve any negative energy or situation. This candle is excellent for cleansing your altar too, and any well-equipped devotee should keep a white candle in their arsenal, even if it is but a generic one. Along with *las siete potencias*, it is one of the candles that is the most versatile. It can be combined with any other colored candles or in combination with any Santa Muerte statue to bring positivity into a situation. While all gifts are welcome, in particular you can choose to give *la Niña Blanca* white roses and other ivory blooms, white foods such as coconut and white bread or buns, silver tequila (known as *blanco*, which means "white"), mezcal, and copal.

Interesting combinations you can try are white in tandem with bone-colored Santa Muerte for healing bones or related injuries. White also pairs positively with silver Saint Death and copper Bone Mother, but in reality with a white candle by itself, you can never go wrong. In Mexico, plain white candles in glass are sold everywhere, and in the US too, they are easy to find and cheap, so an excellent choice for the thrifty practitioner. These plain, low-cost white candles are used by many devotees as a less expensive option than the "official" Santa Muerte white votive. The white candle is, of course, the perfect one to light when commencing your journey with Most Holy Death and at any time you want to thank her for bringing so much into your life.

Yellow

Yellow candles are excellent for solving problems of all sorts; they symbolize Santa Muerte's power to bring success to us. In Mexico, they are often used for financial aid, as they overlap with the gold, bringing in economic well-being. They can also be used for success in gambling. In Mexico, this is often in cockfights, which are a popular pastime for men, but for the wealthy abroad, they might be used in trading stocks on economic markets or playing roulette. Yellow votives can also be used to reinforce self-confidence and to open our minds to creativity. They promote communication at all levels, from the personal to the spiritual. They can also be used to open doors and draw good luck. As described elsewhere, yellow pairs well with other colors, especially green, white, and blue, to open roads, bring justice, and draw money. A yellow statue with a yellow candle brings a strong energy of success to your altar, home, and life. Yellow candles in general can be paired with any candle where the goal is to obtain victory and achievement, such as in an exam; you might burn blue (for focus) with yellow, and perhaps additionally, a white for light. Yellow, white, and amber are also an excellent trio for the addict seeking to stop gambling, drinking, or taking drugs, although amber alone will work for this too. Excellent offerings are yellow fruits, flowers, and libations such as sunflowers, yellow dahlias, bananas, yellow corn, tortilla chips, golden loaves of bread or buns, blond beer, and golden tequila.

Multicolored, or Seven-Colored

The multicolored candle, known as the *siete potencias* (seven powers), brings multiple interventions on all fronts from Santa Muerte, allowing you to tap into all her powers and virtues to align destiny in your favor and bring luck to all aspects of your life. The multicolored candle is an excellent way to receive the blessings of each color without the need for several candles on your altar. It brings luck in love, health, wealth, justice, concentration and studies, purity, and the spiritual realm. General offerings can be given with the seven-colored candle, including buns; corn; tequila, mezcal, or beer; flowers of multiple colors; and candy or chocolate.

Lesser-Known Candles That Often
Feature Color Combinations

Abre Camino (Road Opener)

Usually, a white, yellow, and blue layering of wax features in the *abre camino* (the road opener) candle. This is an excellent multipurpose candle that you can use alone or that you can pair with any other candle when you feel things are blocked, to increase your chance of getting what you need. Santa Muerte will, through this candle, open up your road for you. For example, if you need money but feel that there are obstacles, light both a gold candle and an *abre camino*. Or if you need legal help but again find that obstacles are preventing a successful and fair trial, light a green candle alongside this one. Any obstacle—whether in love, money, health, or wealth—can be dealt with by using this candle, alone or in combination with others to open up paths. It is also excellent when you need new job opportunities to open up for you, or you require an alternative solution to open up to you as the options available to you are unsatisfactory.

Amarre de Pies y Manos (Binding of Feet and Hands)

The *amarre de pies y manos* candle is useful for stopping someone from taking action that may harm you, your family, or your business. Say someone is threatening to take legal action against you or to report your actions to a boss or otherwise cause you trouble through their actions; in that case, light this candle. This will tie their hands and feet so that they can take no action against you.

Ciega, Sorda y Muda (Blind, Deaf and Mute)

The *ciega, sorda y muda* candle is used in cases where you need strong protection from enemies, rivals, and traitors. It is ideal for the Sicario Prayer in chapter six. The candle will ensure that your enemies do not see you (thanks to Saint Death's powerful mantle covering your activities), prevent them from talking about you, and stop them from spreading malicious gossip about you. It is useful for court cases or issues with the police, and can be combined with the green candle and the black candle or the reversible candle for extra protection. This candle is also an excellent choice in any situation of tension—for example, to deal with a toxic workplace, a difficult family member, nasty neighbors, or gossip-mongering acquaintances.

Cordero Manso (Meek Lamb)

Cordero manso, also known as *corderito manso*, candles often come in blue and red layers, but I have seen other colors, or just red. This powerful candle is used in Mexico to make a loved one meek and mild as a lamb, compliant, sweet, and kind. It is helpful in abusive relationships. The candle is said to soften your lover's heart so that they obey, listen, care, and cooperate with you and become a wonderful, loving partner. It is helpful in situations where you need Santa Muerte to intervene to help calm down your lover; to make them less angry, less argumentative, and less mean. Light this candle next to the photo of your beloved beside it and pray to Santa Muerte to bring peace and happiness to your relationship. It can also be used in abusive or difficult work relationships where you need a boss or other person in power to cooperate with you, respect you, and listen to you. In any situation of mistreatment, dealing with difficult personalities, especially with your partner, this is an excellent candle. Offerings can be of pink or red roses, and sweet things such as candy, honey, chocolate, and cinnamon.

Doblegado a mis Pies (Submissive at My Feet)

The *doblegado a mis pies* candle typically features the image of someone on their hands and knees, as another person stands over them, often with a whip in hand, or Santa Muerte stands dominant with her scythe ready to strike them on the bottom. This candle is lit to ask Santa Muerte for total domination, usually of a loved one, but it could also be of a boss or business partner. In general, in Mexico, it is used to get your partner to be totally submissive, sexually and emotionally. Paired with their soiled underwear and a photo of them, this candle inscribed with their initials will make them into your sexual plaything, to do with as you please.

Separa Amantes (Separate Lovers)

The *separa amantes* candle is not usually sold as a Holy Death candle, but I have seen it on altars nonetheless, and it is accepted by la Santa. It is useful for separating your beloved from someone they are cheating on you with, or to make a couple break up.

Tapa Boca (Shut Your Mouth)

The *tapa boca* candle comes in many colors, often green and red, red and black, or fully black, although I have seen other hues. Use it when you need someone to stop spreading malicious gossip about you, smearing your name, leaking your secrets, talking nonsense, or being argumentative at every turn. It is excellent in legal situations, when combined with the green candle, to shut up witnesses or at work to get that boss or coworker to quit whining all day. We have all encountered people who would do best to zip their lip; this candle will keep them quiet.

Ven Dinero (Money, Come to Me)

Usually, a yellow layer and a green layer of wax constitute the *ven dinero* candle, which is used to open roads to gain financial success. Offerings should follow suit. This can be combined with pure gold candles.

Chile Candle

The chile candle will knock out your enemies with a spicy blow, shutting up the envious, gossip-mongers, troublesome neighbors, and people who generate bad vibes.

Reversible, Black and Red

The reversible candle is perfect for sending back evil energy and bad luck to the sender. It is a safer bet than the black candle, as lighting it calls on Santa Muerte to boomerang back all ill to the one who caused it, without the risk of things turning back to bite you in the behind. When someone hexes you, knowingly or unknowingly, with an evil eye or malevolent magic, this candle will return that evil to them. It is always black and red, and the potency with which it will send back that malevolence will be indicated on the label. I have seen two times, three times, and even seven times. This refers to the multiple with which that evil energy will be boomeranged back to the sender. If you sense that someone is constantly creating trouble for you and wishing you harm, hurt, and ill will, use the reversible candle to ensure that anything they send your way goes right back to them. Keep lighting candles until Santa Muerte gives them a massive spiritual knockout punch.

33 Essencias (Thirty-Three Essences)

Said to bring triple luck, the *33 essencias* candle is used to invoke positive energy at all levels. Its combination of thirty-three essences attracts pure and positive energy. It is recommended in any situation where you need extra luck, love, family, peace, studies, work, and money.

Supercharging Candles

Candles may be prepared and supercharged before lighting them with powders or oils. I particularly recommend supercharging them if you are working *brujeria* (witchcraft). I will list only a few of the powders and oils here, since there are so many. Pair your candle with the matching item to make it extra potent. You can use Holy Death powder, known as *polvo Santa Muerte*, for any petition that you wish to add supplementary strength to. *Polvo doble suerte* (double luck powder) will increase the odds of success of a petition where good fortune is required. *Polvo gana juicio* is used to a win court case. *Polvo destruccion* is used in dark *brujeria* to destroy an enemy. Both *arrasa todo* and *triangulo magico* are said to get rid of all bad energy. *Jorobado humillador* serves to humiliate enemies. *Polvo jala jala* (come to me) and *toloache* (made from the plant angel's trumpet) are sprinkled atop candles to draw your love to you. Gold flakes can also be used to attract money on gold and yellow candles. Chile flakes can be peppered atop candles to injure enemies. *Polvo perro cazador* (hunting dog powder) can be used on a candle to drive away troublesome bad neighbors. *Tripas del Diablo* (Devil's Guts) is used to cure addictions, such as alcoholism or drug abuse, and is perfect atop an orange candle.

Innumerable oils exist, and some devotees use them to empower their votives. *Aceite Santa Muerte* (Santa Muerte oil) is used to strengthen the petition of any votive. *Aceite gallina negra* (black hen oil), which can also be bought as a *polvo*, serves to work against the evil eye, malevolent magic, and hexing. *Aceite coyote* (coyote oil) is used to dominate a situation. It is traditionally made from infusing coyote fur in oil to extract its powers. I know of a *bruja* who makes her own, as she knows the location of a coyote den where she collects fur to suffuse in oil. Few of us, however, have access to coyote dens; therefore, you may buy this premade oil in any good esoteric store. The coyote is known as a wily and powerful animal in Mexico, and the Aztec had such respect for the animal that they worshiped Huehuecóyotl, a bisexual trickster god who took on the form of a coyote, and was feared and revered for his cunning and known for his uninhibited sexuality. Coyote oil is used in *brujeria* to dominate others amorously and in prayers of lust and sex. For example, it is employed to make someone you love leave the person they are with and come to you and is often used in combination with a *ven a mi* (come to me) or a red Santa Muerte candle. But people also use it in situations where they need more power and protection from danger, such as to take control in a business situation or in malevolent magic where trickery and deceit are required. While this book focuses on Mexican praxis, I should note that upon a trip to the US, I saw Mexican-American devotees using it to dominate and evade Jonny Law, some anointing their skin with it to protect themselves and their family from the police.

Another oil that is made via infusion is *esencia pajaro macua*. This is made by steeping a macaw's nest in oil. While some people in Mexico even pray to the bird, many simply anoint their candles with it and potentially their skin. I am wary of purchasing this, as macaws were once numerous in Mexico, but today there are few of these beautiful birds, and I would not want to disturb their nests. The colorful birds can now be found only in Oaxaca and Chiapas, where some *curanderos* still hand-steep the essence. Nevertheless, this oil is popular, and that on sale mostly comes from Venezuelan sources. There are many legends surrounding the macaw. Some say that the bird has a special place in God's heart, as it was the macaw who came to Jesus's aid, removing the thorns of the crown nailed to his forehead during his crucifixion. Others state that the bird has incredible positive magnetism and brings speed to spells and petitions, as the macaw is known for its high-speed flight. It is said that the bird makes its nest only in the highest peaks, thus attracting high and positive vibrations. This oil is used in prayers that require luck, good fortune, and positive energy—in particular, love petitions but also related to health, finances, and luck.

Interpreting the Flame

Another aspect of *brujeria* I learned of in Mexico is how to interpret the candle flame. While many know a bright, strong flame means success is sure and a withering flame is an ill omen or means a petition will take a long time to come through, many fail to observe or understand the many other movements and patterns a flame may form. This guide I present to you is a collection of the knowledge I have acquired from years of study with *curanderos* and witches.

When the point of the flame burns bright and strong

The petition will be heard.

When the flame is small

The petitioner needs to have patience; results will take a long time.

When the flame releases sparks

This indicates that you could have some kind of disappointment before your petition is fulfilled.

When the flame rises and falls

This indicates that you are thinking several things at the same time; your mind is confused. You need to find focus.

When the flame wavers and vacillates

There will be changes in your life, and things will not turn out as you wish.

When the flame flickers to the right

The answer to your question is yes, or the solution to your problem will soon be clarified. This portends quick solutions in the life of the person who consults.

When the flame flickers to the left

The answer to your question is no. This is a good time to plan things but not to carry out actual plans.

When the wick won't light or lights with difficulty

If, when you're lighting the candle, the match goes out too early or the candle simply does not want to light, then your environment or aura is charged with bad energy; something is working against you. Do a cleanse and clean your altar before starting again.

When the candle will not stay lit despite repeatedly trying to light it

Your petition will not be heard. There is too much energy blockage. Cleanse and start afresh.

When the candle goes out by itself after burning for a long time with no apparent reason

When the flame, after burning for a long time, goes out without the presence of obvious air currents but before the candle is finished, this means the hardest part of your prayer will be answered, and you have Santa Muerte's blessing for your desire. But much of what you ask will have to be achieved by you alone through hard work, sacrifice, and determination.

When the flame looks like a spiral

Your request will be answered, and good news will follow.

When the flame remains static

If the flame is totally still with no oscillation, this augurs stagnation and little action. However, in love, this is positive, as it is associated with stability, emotional peace, tranquility, and calm.

When the flame zig-zags

There is doubt and mistrust, and you may experience a crisis or great problems. Much work needs to be done on yourself and the situation before it can change. Caution is advised.

When the flame becomes two flames

You are at a cross-roads, and there are two possible paths. If the two flames stay separate and small, your path is about to split away from someone else's, but the outcome will be positive. If the two flames are large and burn wildly, you may quarrel with someone and see a parting of ways. There is bad energy, so cleanse yourself. If the two flames come together after being separate, there will be a union with someone and coming together.

When the flame becomes three flames

You are torn between three paths and between heart, body, and mind. Follow your intuition and protect yourself to ensure the right decision is made for your long-term happiness and safety.

Interpreting the Burnt Candle
Jar once the Wax Is Gone

The sides of the glass are totally blackened

There is much negative energy around you; possibly someone is sending you evil energy. A deep cleanse with herbal baths is recommended of yourself, your altar, and your statues. More candles should be burnt until the glass is clear to ensure your petition is fulfilled as negative energy is blocking your path. It is highly advised to burn candles for protection, or use the reversible candle.

The sides of the glass are somewhat blackened

There is some negative energy around you. A small cleanse using incense or tobacco is recommended for your altar and your statues, and one more candle should be burnt.

The sides of the glass are clear

Your projects will go well. You have Santa Muerte's blessing. Nothing stands in your way.

The sides of the glass are white

Spiritual presence is active on your altar; you have supreme blessings from la Santa.

The candle glass cracks

If your candle jar cracks while burning, always put it out and throw the candle away. There is evil and envy working against you; people wish you harm, but Santa Muerte, through the candle, has taken the blow for you and your petition will be burnt. Be sure to cleanse yourself and be cautious. If it cracks and the jar is clean, all will be well. If it cracks and the jar is blackened, beware. There is evil working against you.

Interpreting Symbolism in the Remains of Your Candle Wax

Ceromancy is one of the most ancient and occult types of divination and a secret method to augur the future. It is essential to proper practice and portending events. Here is a guide to help you understand your wax remains.

Ant: There is envy around you; be careful.

Apple: Take advantage of a favorable opportunity; do not let it escape.

Axe or scales: Legal problems, paperwork issues.

Baby: A new project will give fruit, or you will get pregnant.

Birds: Inspiration and creativity.

Book: Make use of information and knowledge wisely, and all will go in your favor.

Bow and arrow: Although your weapons are not the best, with intelligence, you can fight for what you want.

Broom: It is time to clean your aura and your environment of negative energy, bad habits, and nefarious people.

Candle: The solution to your problems lies elsewhere—for example, in another city or in another activity or with someone you have not turned to as yet.

Circle with dots: Success is assured.

Claw: A warning of danger.

Cloud: Be careful; others wish to dampen your plans.

Crown: Success, financial luck, progress in the workplace, and recognition.

Crutch: It is necessary to find the support of friends.

Diamond shape: Take advantage of this moment to make plans and put your goals into action, as everything will go in your favor.

Dog: Turn to loyal friends for support.

Dove: Peace and positivity in work and your spiritual life.

Dragon: Forces are too formidable against you. Wait a few months and try again.

Egg: Uncertain success and a probable confrontation between two people.

Elephant: Slow and steady is the best way to achieve your goals.

Envelope: New information will come to light that may have unintended consequences or cause you to have a change of heart.

Flower: Projects will bloom for you.

Grasshopper: Look before you leap.

Half moon: Emotional moments of sadness and tears.

Hammer: It is time to settle on your goals and purpose in life.

Hands or fingers: You will receive help from a relative or friend.

Heart: Love will come into your life; you are loved.

Horn: An important trip or an important purchase.

Horse: A trip or journey, favorable business propositions, or pleasant work.

House: Economic well-being for you and your family.

Key: The doors are open. Do not miss the opportunity.

Man: The help and/or the protection of an important friend.

Mortar: Hard work is necessary to achieve your goals.

Numbers: Numbers must be interpreted in a temporal sense; they could indicate days, months, or years until your petition is heard or could be advice on when to take action. You will have to use your best judgment.

Owl: Death is coming, but this could also be metaphorical, as in something is ending for something new to begin. Could also augur communication with Santa Muerte.

Pen: Plan things before proceeding; calculate everything.

Rat: People want to take advantage of your good nature, or that of the person for whom the candle was lit.

Raven: An omen of bad news, but Santa Muerte will protect you if you turn to her.

Rays: A lot of gossip and slander around you.

Rooster: An imminent betrayal. If you are going to travel, postpone the trip; if you are about to sign a contract or other business document, wait.

Santa Muerte: You have the Powerful Lady's full support.

Scepter: An important event will bring you recognition and new power; this could be a promotion in your career or recognition in your profession.

Scythe: There is an imminent halt to your projects, or you need to cut something/someone from your life. Ask Santa Muerte for aid.

Snail: Happiness in family life and security.

Snake: Traitors in your midst, malicious people, and gossipers.

Starfish: From the troubled waters; if you know how to take advantage of the situation, you will benefit.

Stick: Unexpected help and support.

Secrets of Santa Muerte

Sun: Success assured in your projects, if they have a good foundation.

Sword: All success will be at the cost of your effort and hard work.

Table: An important meeting will take place, possibly in business. Be careful.

Throne: Your reputation will improve, and you may also get a new job with sure success.

Trees: Projects will begin to have good foundations and solid roots.

Triangle: Obstacles and troubles.

Two semi-circles: Your plans will come to fruition with perseverance and hard work.

Watch: It is time to make serious decisions about the future.

Wheel: Difficulty with progress; hard work necessary to advance.

Woman: Count on a female figure in your life.

Final Note

When Santa Muerte comes through for you, you should always thank her with a gift, especially if you have promised her something. But either way, when using the prayers in the next chapter or with a spell in the one after that, when she answers you with a miracle, blessings, or even vengeance, you must thank her with offerings. Flowers, alcohol, food, and incense/tobacco are always well received. For the devotee who has decided to dedicate themselves to Death for life, you may also offer her at the time of a vital petition a tattoo that you will have inked on a chosen body part if she comes through. This is one of the, if not the highest, forms of offering to la Santísima Muerte. Some devotees say these tattoos also offer protection from danger. Tattoos are for life, and you will even take them with you into the grave when you are reunited once and for all with Death herself.

CHAPTER SIX

Prayers

The prayers in this chapter are all collected from across Mexico, so they are of utmost authenticity. I have heard them being recited in shrines, found them in prayer books I have been gifted by Santa Muerte devotional leaders, or been gifted them by *curanderos, brujos,* or devotees. They exist only in Spanish; therefore, I have given my best translation, seeking to create rhyming phrases when this existed in the Spanish form to retain as much of the lyrical and magical character of the language as possible. I have done my utmost to keep all content as close to the original as possible without losing the intention, and if the language is at times archaic, it is because some of these prayers are old.

Prayers must always be accompanied by candles. Choose your colors wisely, as outlined in the preceding chapter. Offerings should also be given when you are asking Santa Muerte to come through on a favor, and gifts furthermore promised, then offered if Santa Muerte comes through on your petition. Some prayers require that you recite "Our Father, who art in Heaven" or "Our Father, Be Glory" at the end of them. These prayers can be found online or in a Bible.

I have featured several prayers for the same topic so that you can choose which is best for your needs. Some of these prayers are well known, but a few, especially those for hexing, love, and justice, are recondite and known to few. Such hexes and love spells are extremely powerful and not to be used lightly. As stated previously, malevolent magic has consequences. If, for example, someone owes you money, it is best not to hex them if you think they can still pay up, or your relations with them may sour so deeply that they may never repay you, especially as their life falls apart around them. It would therefore be best, if you want your money back, to use the "So That Debtors Pay Up" prayer. However, if the person has disappeared with your money forevermore with no chance of return, then a hex is not out of place.

Likewise, love magic is powerful, and both prayers and spells have consequences. Be sure you truly want this person in your life as they may be hard to cut loose once you have bewitched them, and you may realize at this point that they are not the cat's pajamas. Pick and choose your spiritual battles carefully. Those who are truly, deeply devoted to death do not ask her to intervene at the drop of a hat on the most mundane issues; rather, they pray daily in her honor with no ulterior motive and ask for her to intervene only when they truly require her deathly power for serious matters. One last point is to personalize your prayers, with the exception of the rosary. The petitions often contain spaces where you can ask exactly what you want or name a person whom you wish to influence. I advise that you make prayers your own by adding personalized words to Santa Muerte within them; this brings potency to them and makes them more likely to be heard than rote repetition.

Novenas

For your prayers to be most powerful, buy a nine-day Santa Muerte candle, and do a novena, a nine-day prayer. Light your candle beforehand, recite the prayer, leave the candle burning—if you can—for nine days, and recite the same prayer nine nights in a row. If you cannot leave the nine-day candle burning unattended, then just light it every time you pray. On the ninth day, the last one of prayer, keep the candle burning until it goes out.

Nightly and Daily Prayers

Daily Prayer 1

O Santísima Muerte,
Relic of God,
Rid me of my sorrows.
As you protect me at my side.
May your endless desire
For doing what is good,
Be with me always
Bringing me blessings
No matter what anyone says or does.
With your sacred scales,
Your celestial sphere,
And your holy mantle
May you cover me always,
Santísima Muerte.
Amen.

(Repeat every day of the Novena.)

Daily Prayer 2

Santísima Muerte,
Beloved Lady,
Mistress of all that is obscure and cold,
I come to implore you for your protection.
Powerful Lady,
Care for me and keep me safe from my enemies,
From those who wish to deceive, trap, or reap vengeance upon me.
Cover me with your mantle of invisibility
So that no unhappy accident may befall me.
O Holy Death,

You who can see even in the deepest darkness,
Please take care of me, my house, and family.
In the name of the Father, the Son, and the Holy Ghost.
Amen.

Daily Rosary to Santa Muerte

The rosary is used in Santa Muerte as a form of prayer offering to the Powerful Lady to open doors to her and to meditate upon her deeply. It can take as long or as little time as you want, but ideally it is for longer, deeper prayer. I have not included the longer ten-page rosary that many devotees recite in Mexico due to limited space. When doing the rosary, you will need a Santa Muerte rosary necklace of fifty-nine beads. Start at the medallion of Santa Muerte, and then with your fingers, move along the necklace one bead at time, and reciting one word per bead, go around the rosary at least three times. You may choose to recite the rosary many more times and, in so doing, enter into a deep, meditative, trance-like state where you may meet Death deep in the realm of the sacred.

O Santa Muerte, Beloved Death!
I prostrate myself before your divine presence,
Asking you to grant me permission to spend a few minutes of my time,
Praying a Holy Rosary to you Santa Muerte,
Our godmother and protector.
You are the only one who understands and embraces me,
In the moments of greatest need and sadness.
I am happy to carry your grace and love in my heart,
Santa Muerte, you who bring peace and harmony to my life,
You who break the chains that incite me to wrongdoing,
Forgive me for anything I may have done,
And guide me into the arms of our Lord.
My Santa Muerte,
Who was the companion of the Son of God,
I beg you that all my wrongs be forgotten.
Beloved Death,

Do not allow anguish and sadness to invade my heart,
Drive away my enemies and protect the people I love.
Only in you can I trust,
You know my heart and my needs.
I thank you for the opportunity,
I have to praise you dear Death daily.
Amen!

Prayer of the Night

Precious Santa Muerte,
You who are always with me.
Even as I lie in bed slumbering,
You continue to hold my resting body.
I am not aware of the processes
That continue in my body in deep sleep,
But you know every cell in my body,
And I ask that in safety you my body keep.
While I sleep, help me to leave behind
Today's problems and unwind,
Let me forgive and forget momentarily
those who have hurt and wronged me.
When I wake up, let me recall
That my mistakes have been forgiven,
Both big and small,
And that you always take care of me,
Whether my eyes are open or closed,
Unconditionally.
Santa Muerte, you never sleep or rest,
But look after us constantly.
My need to rest and sleep
Reminds me of my limited existence, my mortality.
But you, Beloved Death,

Have no limits,
Not to your power nor majesty.
I trust you while I sleep
Because you never stop taking care of me
And my loved ones incessantly.
As we lie in our beds,
All my secrets you keep.
Most precious Santa Muerte,
Continue to protect me and care always.
You are faithful to all your promises
And I too shall be faithful to you for all my days
And keep all my promises to you,
Santa Muerte, who is omniscient, omnipotent, and true.
I thank you for the gift of the day
Which is now ending.
I pray you forgive me for anything
That I might have done wrong
And keep me safe
All night long.
I commit my whole being to you,
Mind, body, and soul.
Take care of me while I sleep,
Protect me from evil and sorrow,
Equip me with the strength I need for tomorrow,
Generous Santa Muerte,
My whole life is a gift from you.
When another day ends,
I place myself again at the foot of the cross,
Where I am forgiven and cleansed
By the blood of Jesus
And your power which all transcends.
It is here where I find rest and restoration.
So to you I humbly pray,

I thank you for the blessings of today,
The refreshing air, the sunlight, moments of satisfaction
The food I have enjoyed, the interactions
that I have had with other people,
and all other successful transactions.
You have blessed me
Beyond the limits of my comprehension,
Removing from me misapprehension.
O Beloved Death,
Thanks for the mercy you have shown me today
And for your generosity and grace.
Free me from everything that keeps me awake.
Take me to a pleasant and peaceful place of rest.
You who have the power to defeat all evil,
To you I give all my faith, O Holy Death.
Amen.

Prayer to la Niña Blanca

(Light a white candle.)

Niña Blanca,
You who are the guardian of the lost souls in Purgatory,
You who are the protector of all mortals born of this land,
Niña Blanca,
Today I come before you to seek your mercy and charity.
Kneeling in front of your image, I invoke your powerful hand.
I implore your full protection from those who wish me ill.
Niña Blanca,
My Mother, I ask you from my heart to hear this humble petition.
(State your request.)
And I beg you to grant me your intercession
Before Almighty God.
I pray you never leave me.

I pray that you remove all barriers and enmity
And all obstacles in front of me,
Opening every door that was closed to me,
And please hold my hand
And guide my steps on the path that you set me on in this land.
I ask all this with total faith from a pure heart,
Always thanking you for all the kindness you impart,
Thank you for all your help and protection
For your guidance and affection.
So be it, and So it will be.
Amen.

Prayer of la Niña Negra

(Offer a black candle.)

Holy Niña Negra,
I approach you with love and devotion.
Your great love and faith ensures that the prayers
Of your devoted children will be heard, granted,
And set in motion.
I pray for your helping hand,
Aid me to understand the decisions
That God for me has planned,
So I can accept
The trials of life
With patience, hope, and with strength all withstand.
Blessed Niña Negra,
Many fear you,
But I love you with a pure heart.
Kneeling before your holy image,
I thank you for the goodness and hope you impart.
Sometimes during this journey
I lose my way,

I get lost and let anguish take away
Peace from my mind, heart, and soul.
The problems I face sometimes overwhelm me,
I feel so forgotten, abandoned, and no longer whole.
Today I come before you,
Just as I am,
Broken and beaten,
Begging for your help and compassion.
Please look at me,
See my piety.
Please, hear my cries of anxiety
And listen to my prayers for your protection
In these times of problems, insecurity, and dejection.
I beg you now, Niña Negra,
That you grant to me,
Your intercession so holy
Before Christ the Redeemer
I whisper my needs to you solely.
(State your request.)
Under your sacred shield,
Help me carry the weight of this load
That the Lord has given me
To carry on this long road
So that one day with you
I can share
The crown of eternal life
When you, Santa Muerte,
Take my soul into the celestial air.
Amen.

Prayer to las Siete Potencias

(Light *las siete potencias* candle.)

Dear Santa Muerte of the Seven powers,
In prayer I present myself to ask
For your sacred protection on my path.
Bless my night and my days,
So that I can achieve success in all ways.
Also help my loved ones, my family.
If at any time they are in jeopardy.
O, Majestic Santa Muerte,
Give me your blessings and shine on me brightly,
And let me receive your seven powers,
Gifted to you by God almighty.
Fill my life with love, harmony,
And restore unity in my family.
May every relationship with them be pleasant and true,
May our connection grow with the same intensity as my
     devotion to you.
Give me clarity for decision making,
So that benefits come to me from every undertaking.
Let me see my income grow as I become a success,
Let me meet my goals as my path you bless.
Most Holy Death of my heart,
May your power and magnificence be present constantly,
So that no evil can ever reach me nor my family.
Protect me from malevolent spirits and protect my soul for eternity.
Cleanse and restore my being with your pure deathly essence,
So that the peace of my heart is never broken thanks to your presence.
Make me worthy of recognizing the good and the bad all around me,
So I may eradicate what does not allow me to advance properly.
Do not allow me to walk in dishonorable ways or treat others
     with roughness

Or do other things that will bring me trouble with justice.
I trust you because your love has been vast.
I thank you for the many blessings that I have received on my path,
And I welcome those miracles that will come to be,
As I receive your seven powers in me.
Amen.

Prayer to Aztec Death

Blessed queen of heaven and earth,
Of death and rebirth,
So beautiful and so loving,
Tender and caring with your faithful devotees,
I come before you full of desperation and unease.
In this valley of tears I pray for your mercy,
Sacred white protector of the Holy Trinity.
Lower your gaze upon me, your faithful child in these dark times,
I am lost, so help me my path to find.
Goddess and Aztec Queen,
Given the greatest power over all mortal beings.
I call your name Niña Blanca, Niña Blanca, Niña Blanca.
Ensure justice for me at all times,
Always protect me from distress, danger, and crime,
I ask you to bless my house, my beloved and me,
With gifts of good health, wealth, success, abundance, good fortune,
*   and prosperity.*
I ask you to bless me with constant, honest work.
Please remove all poverty and financial difficulty.
Cover my home with your Holy Mantle,
Form a shield around my loved ones and me.
Saint and Aztec Queen,
Your strength and power opens doors,
And fulfills dreams.

There is no one that will escape you,
So I place all my trust in your bony hands
And on your cold skeletal lap I rest,
Because I know you are always with me on my path to death.
Your power will clear any obstacle that blocks my way
And all favors will be granted upon my humble request.
I offer with all my soul and heart this modest candle to you,
With my devotion and my love which will be forever true.
Amen.

Prayers of Thanks

Prayer of Thanks to Santa Muerte

Almighty God, I thank you for leading me to Santa Muerte.
O Santa Muerte, Mother of Mine, I thank you for all the help you
give me and give us all who ask with love; I ask you never to
leave my side, to take care of the path I tread, and to care for all
my family and all the beings I love.
O Santa Muerte, forgive me if I sometimes despair, doubt, or distrust,
But I never doubt you! But sometimes fear and doubt the people
around me. Forgive me if I ever distrust your great power.
Santa Muerte, Mother of Mine, I can always count on you when
my enemy is near or when the pain I feel is very great. My
Mother, please never forget that I exist, and always be with me
everywhere I go, and everywhere I go, defend me from all those
who want to hurt me.
My Mother, grant me the blessing of seeing you even in my dreams,
And I will never forget that what I once thought so far from me is
now close to me; to see you, hear you, and have you in my life
makes me the happiest mortal the Creator has ever given life to.

I thank you, my Mother, for taking care of my path and all those
dear to me.
In the name of the Father, the Son, and the Holy Spirit.
Amen.

Prayer of Gratitude

O Santa Muerte,
Powerful Skeletal Spirit,
Your bounteousness is vast
Your intervention is efficient.
Humbly, I thank you for all you have done for me.
I thank you for your spiritual favors, that you promised and gave me.
I thank you and ask you
That you keep protecting me
Me and (name anyone else you wish to protect)
I name you my advocate,
And I hope my advocate you will remain,
That no one may harm me,
And if they seek to send me evil,
May that be returned unto them.
Thank you, Santa Muerte.
Amen.

Prayers for Love

Oldest Prayer for Love (Dating Back at Least Fifty Years)

Most Dearest Death of my Heart,
Protect me, please,
And do not give (person's name),
A moment of peace.
Make him/her restless all the time,

And worried about me,
Until she/he is mine.
(Recite three Our Fathers.)

Prayer for Love 1

Santa Muerte of my Heart,
Give me your divine protection always,
And do not let as of this moment (person's name)
Have any desire, have any plans but to be with me.
That his/her love, his/her affection, his/her caresses and kisses be
*   all for me.*
For all the gifts that you have granted me,
I will overcome all obstacles,
And love and illusion will not interfere with my veneration of you.
May everything that I aspire to, want, or propose to do, bring me
*   absolute success.*
And please bring to me the one I adore.
With these divine powers that God gave you, I believe in God
And in you, forevermore,
My Santa Muerte.

Prayer for Instant Love

Lady of the darkness,
Make it so that at this very moment (person's name) thinks of me,
Wanting to be by my side at all costs, wanting to see me, hug and hold me,
May their mouth be excited to kiss me, their body long to be entwined
*   with mine,*
And make it so that in their thoughts are only thoughts of me.
May (person's name) seek me now and call me to be by their side forever.
Pretty lady, I beg you to grant me this right now,
In their thoughts, in their being, may they only feel desire for me.
With your infinite power, make it so, make them love me infinitely,

I have faith in you,
Let this be fulfilled forevermore.
Beloved Death, whom I adore.
Amen.

Prayer for Impossible Love

O Holy Death,
Love has knocked on my door, but dear Santa Muerte,
She/he has been capricious with me,
I find myself dejected because I love, but my love is not requited.
The suffering of powerlessness seizes me.
I see that I do not have in my hands the solution to my problem.
I implore you with great sadness in my heart to hear my prayer.
I hope you listen and feel how my being beats when my love is talking.
The person I love is an impossible love,
But I want the miracle of having them by my side.
That is why I come to you,
You who are kind and miraculous.
I want that person to become my partner
And for my love to be reciprocated.
I will be infinitely grateful to you.
I am a faithful believer in you.
I beg you.
And will wait the time necessary for my request to be fulfilled.
While I wait, I will prove my loyalty by giving my offerings to you
And for a long time, my dear Santísima Muerte.
O Holy Death,
I trust in you and put all my faith in you,
I hope you listen to me and fulfill my wish.
So be it.
Amen.

No Other Woman but Me

(*Man* and *woman* can be changed where necessary for the male petitioner.)

Body and soul of
(The name of the loved one is said),
You will not want nor see
Any other woman but me.
Santa Muerte,
Bring him to me!
Sweet Lady with your mighty spirit,
Bring him to me!
Niña Roja, bring him to me
(The name of the loved one is said).
Amen.

Prayer for Protection from an Abusive Ex and to Find New Love

Santa Muerte Red Lady,
Protect me from a lover who would not wish me well,
Who would use and abuse me.
Drive them away always,
And ensure that in my life,
I am always blessed by the love of those
Who wish the best for me, my health, well-being, and heart happiness.
Thank you.
Amen.

Prayer to Dominate and Bind a Lover

Burning affection, burning passion.
I feel for you (person's name)
And you feel for me.
Your thoughts and your feelings
I dominate them totally.

Your mind and your actions are totally controlled
By the influence of Santísima Muerte
Who owns your soul.
I call you (person's name),
I need you (person's name),
Come find me (person's name),
And bowed before me you will be (person's name).
Show me all your love (person's name),
Kneel at my feet.
Do everything I ask of you.
Lady of the Night,
Dominant lady of the universe,
And of its earthly energies;
Influence and dominate the mind
The actions and heart of (person's name).
Dominant lady,
You, my Santa Muerte,
Bring to me (person's name),
Tamed before me.
May your feet bring you to me,
May your heart gush with love for me,
May your body ache for me,
May your passion flow endlessly for me.
My Santa Muerte,
Do not give a minute of pleasure or tranquility
to (person's name) if they are not with me.
Do not let any other woman/man get within proximity,
And if they approach them,
Send them packing for eternity.
If they are not for me, let them be nobody's.
Santísima Muerte, Mighty Lady,
I ask you with all my devotion
That you give me (person's name).

Myrtle sap flows burning through their blood.
I call you (person's name) come to me.
Your heart, your thoughts, and your body
From this moment they are
And will be mine for eternity.
In the name of Blessed Death,
I ask you,
Dominant Lady, bring me (person's name).
Make him/her drunk with love for me.
Bring them surrendered kneeling at my feet,
Submissive to all my wishes eternally
And desperate to show me their love.
Santísima Muerte,
You who move all energies,
Even the densest and most difficult in the universe,
Make (person's name) surrender to me.
I ask you to bring them to me with your power divine,
Wherever they may be.
Be it from the darkest recesses,
Or the farthest reaches,
always put (person's name)
In front of me
So that their path crosses mine.
Santísima Muerte, you who can be a thousand,
You, who can be a million,
You, who are immortality,
Bring me (person's name)
Madly in love with me.
I ask that your deathly stallion bring them to me.
Let your scythe drag him/her to me.
And Powerful Lady, make sure that even if I'm not with him/her,
They imbibe my scent, recall me,
So that I am present in their mind

No matter who they are with
Or where they are
All the time.
Lady of the Night,
Lady of the Day,
To you, I pray,
I ask you that the spirit
Of (person's name)
Longs to be with me in every way,
That she/he only loves me
And only has eyes for me.
Santísima Muerte, work your magic to bind (person's name)
to my heart, my body, and my soul
For all eternity.
(Person's name), come to me.
By night and by day, you will be with me.
Please, I ask you
In the name of Holy Death and all creation.
Santísima Muerte, give me his/her love,
Give me the strength
And total domination
Of (person's name).
Santísima Muerte,
I beg you to be my protector
And fulfill all petitions of mine
Until the last day of time
When your divine majesty
Orders me,
Before your deathly presence.
I call upon you, Santísima Muerte.
Don't abandon me, Santísima Muerte.
Don't ignore me, Santísima Muerte.
Santísima Muerte, bring me (person's name).

Santísima Muerte, bring me (person's name).
Santísima Muerte, bring me (person's name).

Return a Wayward Lover: Novena, Nine-Day Prayer

First Day

Holy Death,
I beseech you lovingly inasmuch as Immortal God created you with
*   your great power over all mortals.*
So that you might place them in the celestial sphere where we may
*   enjoy a glorious day without night for all eternity.*
That in the name of the Father and the Son and the Holy Spirit,
You be my protector, and grant me all the favors I ask of you in
*   this Novena,*
Until the last day, hour, and moment of time,
When your divine majesty commands me before your presence.
Amen.

(Recite three Our Fathers.)

Second Day

Jesus Christ, conqueror who on the Cross was overcome,
Conquer the heart of (insert name of the beloved)
Let he/she be overcome by me,
In the name of the Lord,
If they are as fierce as a wild animal, make them meek as a lamb,
Render them mild as the Rosemary flower,
They must come.
They ate of my bread, and now they must give this to me.
By your most powerful word, I want you to bring me (person's name).
That he/she be humbled,
kneeling at my feet to fulfill what he/she has promised me.
I beseech you lovingly inasmuch as Immortal God created you with
*   your great power over all mortals.*

So that you might place them in the celestial sphere where we may
enjoy a glorious day without night for all eternity.

That in the name of the Father, the Son, and the Holy Spirit, I pray
and I beseech you,

That you deign to be my protectress.

And that you grant all the favors that I ask of you,

Until the last day, hour, and second in which your Divine Majesty
commands to take me before your presence.

Amen.

(Recite three Our Fathers.)

Third Day

Jesus Christ, conqueror, in the name of sweetest Jesus, and you most
Holy Death,

Shine upon me your light and fill me with joy,

Bringing me the love of (person's name) whether it be night or day.

I ask you to wield the titanic power that God gifted you with,

I ask that you place me in the heart of (person's name),

That they have no eyes but for me.

Please grant me the favor I ask with this Novena,

Through the power of Santa Muerte and our Lord Jesus Christ.

Amen.

(Recite Our Father, Be Glory.)

Fourth Day

O Santa Muerte,

You that redeemed the Saints,

That led them as sheep because you so desired,

I ask you with all my heart, just as God formed you immortal, mighty
above all mortals,

To grant me this miracle, for me alone, with the great power you have

Make it so that (person's name) cannot have peace of mind, nor eat a
meal, nor sit quietly in a chair,

Until she/he is humbled and kneeling at my feet,

And that she/he will never ever be far from me,

I ask you through the power of the Holy Trinity of the Eternal Father.

Amen.

(Recite three Our Fathers.)

Fifth Day

O Santa Muerte of Jesus, my beloved,

O Sovereign Lady!

You to whom our Eternal Father gave the power to end the lives of
*   all mortals,*

You to whom all come sooner or later,

No matter our riches or our age,

For death comes to us all young, old or child,

You to whom all paths lead when God thus decides,

Santa Muerte, I beg you to make (person's name) fall in love with me,

That they not pay attention to my physical beauty,

Make them discover the goodness of my soul,

And recognize me as their one and only most faithful and constant love.

Amen.

(Recite three Our Fathers.)

Sixth Day

O Santa Muerte!

Glorious and Powerful Death;

You who watch over me at all times,

Make it so that my love thinks of me and only me,

Holy Death, Immortal Lady,

Make it so (person's name) cannot enjoy their walks without me,

Cannot eat without me,

Nor sleep without me by their side,

And that their volition belongs to me,

And that they give me great happiness with their infinite love for me.

Amen.

(Pray three Our Fathers.)

Seventh Day

O Santa Muerte,

Today bring comfort to my heart,

Take away this affliction,

By ensuring my beloved abandon everything

To be with me until death.

Also please deliver me from all evil,

With the immeasurable power that God gave you,

So that we might all enjoy a glorious day without night for
all eternity.

And I ask that you protect me and grant all the favors that I ask of
you in this Novena.

(Make your specific love request).

Amen.

(Recite three Our Fathers.)

Eighth Day

Miraculous and Majestic Death,

I ask that with your immense power you give me the love of
(person's name).

Make it so she/he cannot relax,

Nor enjoy a moment of quiet.

Make it so she/he is unhappy with anyone but me.

Make it so when she/he sleeps she/he dreams of me,

And that when awake all their thoughts are of me.

Make it so that she/he cannot find a moment's rest until she/he
is with me.

I beg you humbly, that their affection, love, life, be mine until death.

Amen.

(Recite Our Father, Be Glory.)

Ninth Day

Please allow me to end my supplications,

Blessed and Protective Death,

With the powers that God gave you;

I ask you to free me from all curses,

From dangers and diseases, and that in return you give me:

Luck, happiness, and money.

I ask you to give me friends and free me from my enemies,

Above all make (person's name) humble before me,

Meek as a lamb, faithful to their promises, loving and submissive to
me for all of this life.

Amen.

(Recite three Our Fathers.)

Prayer to Separate Lovers

(*Separa amantes* is a good candle for this prayer; you can find it online or in botanicas.)

O, Santa Muerte, I come to you to implore you to help me.

I'm disappointed in life.

My best years,

I gave them to a man/woman that I love

But he/she left me for another woman/man.

Punish that woman/man who is hurting me,

Who wants to destroy my marriage.

Keep them away from (loved person's name)

So that he/she will come back to me forever.

Santa Muerte, make (loved person's name)

Start to hate and mistrust her/him,

Realize that they are using her/him,

That all they are after is money and fun,

That they are with my love out of self-interest.

I ask you to separate my beloved

Of everything that takes them away from me,

That the tears shed by me because of this cruel thief of hearts
Become suffering for them (name of person who stole your loved one).
O Holy Death, use your powers to get my love
Out of the clutches of this other woman/man.
Santa Muerte, I ask you to bring (name of loved one)
Right now in front of me.
Bring them back to me meek as a lamb.
Let them forget about (name of the person who stole your loved one).
Make them kneel before me and beg for forgiveness.
O, Santa Muerte, make (name of loved one)
Submit to my wishes.
Make them think of me only.
Let them beg me for mercy and forgiveness.
Let them profess their love for me.
May we be happy again like before.
Do not let me be alone, dearest Santa Muerte.
Amen.

Prayers for Health

Prayer for Health of Someone You Love

Santísima Muerte,
O Lady of Mine,
Angel whom God created to serve and aid,
Today I implore you to heal (person's name)
That their days on earth be many,
That their body regain vigor, strength, and energy.
You who have the power to do anything, save them.
I implore you, and plead you
On this day, at this time,
In the name of Jesus Christ crucified on the Cross,

Please hear my prayer and return them to their home
healthy and well.
Amen.

Prayer for Protection of Your Health

Before this prayer and request, you should light a white candle, burn three sandalwood incense sticks and, if possible, a cigarette, offering them to the Bone Mother as well as one piece of candy, some bread, a glass of water, a glass of her favorite tequila (or mezcal or other libation), and some white flowers.

My Dear Blessed Death, my Beloved Matron Saint,
Thank you so much for everything you do, have done, and continue to
do for me.
I ask you not to let any sick person approach me,
And that, if at some point I am afflicted by a health problem,
Heal me with your immense power,
Because only you can decide who is cured and who dies.
It is not that I am afraid of that moment when I will finally meet you
and be in your bony embrace forever;
I simply enjoy life and what you have given me in life,
And I enjoy my life with you, taking you with me wherever I go.
I enjoy being with those I love and care for,
And I enjoy knowing and experiencing how much the world
has to offer.
That is why I beg you, my Dear Niña Blanca, that should illness
come my way,
You repel it with your scythe,
And should you be unable and I fall ill or am hurt
Help me to heal my wounds and heal any disease that afflicts me,
Because I want to make the most of this life,
As you have taught me and shown me to do.
And I am happy to join you later, when you finally decide I should.

This I ask of you, my Most Holy Death of my life, giving you my
   absolute devotion.
So be it, with your blessing. Stay with me and always let me be at
   your side.
Amen.

Prayer for Healing of Someone Seriously Ill

O blessed Niña Blanca, don't let (person's name)
Be seriously ill.
You who have the power to restore,
Let them regain consciousness and return to a state of well-being,
So that they recognize their family and are able to speak.
Remove that terrible disease that is consuming them.
O Santa Muerte, we beg you to keep them among us, their loved ones,
Give us the solution to your problem so we can help them,
Help (person's name) so that she/he can heal, she/he is young.
Please perform a miracle,
So that she/he recovers and we can be happy again.
Listen to my voice, don't leave me alone.
Santa Muerte, there is nothing that you cannot take away,
So take away that disease,
Give us light and hope so that (person's name) can be saved,
I know that in your heart you will never abandon them.
I beg you to look at them with the eyes of pity.
She/he deserves to live longer,
Grant them the joy of seeing their family grow,
Of being a good person, who longs to live.
Amen.

Prayer for Your Own Healing

(A candle must be lit.)

O Salubrious Santa Muerte,

Today I cry out to you,

To your love and divine wisdom,

So that you cure me of this disease.

I have felt really ill.

Please heal me with your divine power.

These have been hard moments,

And I have seen the end in sight,

But today I ask you to lift me up.

From among all those who are sick, I ask you with faith.

For it is with all the power that is in my heart and my soul that I
*   believe in you.*

O my saint, you are the one who can lift me up,

I prostrate myself before your immense Power.

I pray knowing that only you are able to free me from evil,

And of sickness, with the strength of your love.

Please heal me and get me out of this place of sickness,

For now, and forever.

I will not stop praying to you,

I ask you please give me total healing.

Help me, I beg you.

Please listen carefully to my prayer.

I promise you gifts of (list gifts you will give upon return to health).

Beloved prayer, Holy Death,

Heal me from this sickness,

I beg you on my knees.

Give me relief quickly.

You are the doer of justice.

I pray with all my heart for this disease to be removed from my body.

To you I will give offerings.

Salubrious Santa Muerte,
Raise me up from my sickbed, my Beloved Death.
In my house I will always light a candle for you.
And I will do it as a token of gratitude because I believe in you.
You will save me from being sick.
Amen.

Simple Prayer for Healing

My Dearest, Beloved Santa Muerte,
I thank you for all your bounteousness.
I implore you, Beloved Santa Muerte,
Please look after me and protect me.
Remove all illness from my body,
Alleviate all pain and cure me with your immense power.
So be it!
Amen.

Prayer for Curing Your Sickness and That of Your Family

Dear Santa Muerte, you who hold the secrets of life;
Please end the disease and the pain that has invaded my body and the
*   bodies of those I love.*
Pour a few drops of your magic elixir onto me so that I may return to
*   vigor, lucidity, and strength and continue to adore you. End with*
*   your kind hand the grief that afflicts me and my family. Expel*
*   with your cloak the evil that makes us sick and heal us forever.*
Amen.

Prayer against Coronavirus

Santa Muerte, Lady of the Light,
Before God and before you I kneel so that
You intervene for me and for the entire world
I ask you to eliminate all evil, virus, or bacteria.

Cleanse with your purifying mantle.
Holy Lady, listen to my pleas.
Help and give food and shelter to those who need it
And seek in you strength.
Lady of the End Times, protect us so that we are not infected.
And do not infect those we love
Sweep COVID-19 away from our path
And grant us shelter, food, and support.
I ask you to never fail me.
Amen.

Prayers against Addiction and Vices

Prayer to Break Addictions

Offer one amber, one purple, and one white candle. On all candles, write the name of the person three times with black marker or etch their full name in the wax. Pray and keep praying and offering the candles until the person is clean from their addiction. If you are praying for yourself, follow the same instructions and write your name instead of another's on all candles and say your own name in the prayer.

In the name of the Father, the Son, and the Holy Spirit,
In this moment I beg of you with all my heart
And ask the permission of the Holy Trinity
To invoke the aid and healing power of Santa Muerte.
Mighty and dearest Santa Muerte,
Today, my Mother, I kneel before you
And I beg you, my powerful queen,
Hear this prayer with compassion
And know my piety and devotion.
I ask you in the name of (person's name)
I beg you to remove the chains of addiction from me/he/she,

Sweet Santa Muerte.

I ask you to look down over the body and soul of (name the person
  three times),

And I ask you to cut the binds of this addiction

That holds this mortal being captured in its claws

And lost on its broken path.

I ask you to eliminate the need and desire for alcohol and drugs.

Cure them, clean them from this addiction.

Keep them pure and true,

Make them clean once again, and keep them close to you.

Grant your holy and divine intercession in their name.

In your hands I place this prayer for (person's name).

Remove from them all vice, addiction, and pain.

Amen.

Prayer to Protect Someone from Addictions and Vices

Santa Muerte, Niña Blanca,

My Queen of all the Universe,

You who can do everything and all control

I (your name) ask you from the bottom of my heart and soul

That you keep (person's name) away from vices, and bad ways

With the power you have over all people.

With your Scythe of Justice and of Light, sweep away vices from
  (person's name) for all their days.

Help them, protect them, give them shelter and succor.

Do not let them cause anyone who loves them to suffer.

My Queen, Santa Muerte,

Niña Blanca,

Take the spirit of (person's name).

Move them away from the vice of (name of the vice or vices).

With your miraculous Scythe of Light,

Cut off and take away all the bad friendships and negative influences
that they have around them.
Do not let them be together.
Let them vanish and go away forever and ever.
My Queen and Lady, only you, my Santa Muerte, can do it.
If there is any obstacle for (person's name) to stop (the person's vice,
e.g., doing meth or drinking),
Cut at the root with your scythe of light.
Keep them constantly pure at your side.
I know that with your help they can achieve it,
So be it, so let it be,
and so it will be for all eternity.
Amen.

Prayers for Difficult Cases

Prayer for Difficult Situation

Before you, I come,
My Holy Death,
With the faith of my soul to seek your sacred consolation
In my hard situation.
Let doors open unto me,
Using your powerful scythe to slice them free.
Give me quietness in the place of this anxiety.
If your divine power does not intercede in my favor,
For lack of help, I will succumb to great trouble and failure.
Santa Muerte, powerful and mighty,
Assist me, protect me, and care for me always.
I promise to be your faithful follower
For all of my days.
Amen.

Prayer for Difficult Cases

Mighty Santa Muerte, listen to my prayers,

I need your help. I require your protection in this difficult stage that I am going through (describe the difficult situation) so that you can remedy my ills.

From the bottom of my heart, I beg you please for your support.

Do not leave me alone in these moments because I really need you.

I implore you to purify my heart and eliminate all bad energies that surround me,

So that they do not affect me.

I seek your consolation and the safety of your sacred mantle.

Free me from setbacks that harm me.

Remove from my path any obstacle that stands in my way.

I know that you will listen to my desperate voice, because you feel how much I am suffering.

I ask you to give me the necessary strength to overcome my problems.

In return, I give you my word to (make a promise, offer a gift) and have others invoke you.

Dearest Santa Muerte, thank you for listening to me. So be it.

Amen.

Prayer for Help with a Difficult Job

Santa Muerte, don't let things go wrong.

Let me see the light, let me be strong,

Give me the clarity to think and do the best I can.

Santísima Muerte of my heart,

Allow me to be respected in my job as a capable man/woman.

Give me hope and give me light.

Give me opportunities to show I can do things right.

Do not let me feel discouraged and hopeless.

I ask you with all my heart to help me in my work, to do my best.

Let me enjoy my job

And stop seeing it as a nightmare.
Santa Muerte, please keep me in your constant care.
Take this feeling of defeat away from me,
So I can work hard to support myself and my family.
Amen.

Prayer for Luck

I entrust myself to you, Santa Muerte.
I bring you water and yellow flowers, incense and dirt of this earth.
Please, with your divine power, change the world order,
So that things align so that luck and good fortune favor me and come
    to my path.
Allow causes to have desired effects, keep the flame of fortune alight,
And cut with your scythe the threads of bitterness and bad luck.
Dearest Death, to thank you I will plant trees in the wood and adorn
    your altar with flowers.
I give you these offerings of fruits, so that you make my
    undertakings fruitful.
Amen.

(Note that the offerings mentioned in the prayer and promises must be kept.)

Abre Camino Prayer (Road Opener)

With tears in my eyes, I invoke the powers and strength of
    Santísima Muerte
To overcome and conquer all obstacles in my life and on my path.
I invoke the powers and strength of Santísima Muerte,
To obtain an excellent job that will lead to my success.
I invoke the aid of Santísima Muerte for my life to bless.
To remove all bad luck and misfortune on my road,
I invoke her holiness for good luck and good fortune on my path.
And for my home, I invoke Santa Muerte's powerful protection,

To ensure my path is always safe from danger and harm,
No matter the direction.
I invoke the power of Santa Muerte and her forceful scythe,
So that no danger or occult enemies on my path
Will harm me nor against me connive
I (your name) invoke the miracles and blessings of Santísima Muerte
To obtain abundance, health, well-being, and prosperity.
I (your name) believe in the power of Santa Muerte
And every door and any path that closes unto me,
With her power opened shall be.
So be it and so let it be.
Amen.

Prayer to Make Someone Listen

My Dear Santa Muerte, my Cherished Niña Negra,
Thanking you so much for everything you do, have done, and continue
    to do for me,
I ask you, with your sovereign power, to help me have power over
    (person's name).
I really beg you to make (person's name) listen to me,
Let them listen to me and follow my advice,
Seek my suggestions,
And see in me the only inspiring force they need in their life.
Let every word of mine ring true to (person's name).
Let it be the most obvious and natural word of law that can exist.
I ask you, my dear and esteemed Bony Lady,
That (person's name) recognize in me absolute authority
So that they follow me,
As I follow you
And recognize you as my absolute authority,
Dearest Santa Muerte of my mind, my spirit, and my soul.
This I ask of you, Santísima Muerte of my life,

Giving you my absolute devotion.
So let it be and let it be so,
With your deathly blessing.
Stay with me and always let me be with you.
Amen.

Prayers for Money

Ven Ven Dinero (Money Come to Me)

Money, come come come to me.
I have great faith
For the money will come to me
And will not go away.
This much I want it, so let it be so every day.
Santa Muerte, I greet you,
I worship you, Holy Death.
Give me good luck,
Happiness, love, health,
And a lot of money.
Money, come come come to me,
You will always accompany me
As the good friend you are.
Money, come come come to me.
I need you not to stray too far.
You will arrive by any means
And you will be my great friend for life.
Money, COME COME COME TO ME!

Money Drawing Prayer

Glorious Santísima Muerte,

Most Powerful Lady, faithful friend, and companion on the road,

In whom we trust in all the moments of our hard and difficult
existence, and whom we will all have great happiness to see on
the last day of our life.

You who know the secrets of fortune,

Allow the wheel to turn naturally to where I may benefit the most.

Allow me to partake of your power and please bring me good fortune,
abundance, and prosperity.

Upon your altar I will thank you with great gifts; you, possessor of the
great secrets of luck and fortune, will be honored.

Sweep away, Powerful Lady, with your scythe all those threats
and dangers that hang over me; banish misfortune so that the
brightness that your light confers reaches me.

Provide me with good luck in life and business, may fortune appear at
my door, and may abundance and prosperity reign in my home.

I will thank you with offerings and you will have my fidelity forever.
Thank you, faithful friend and companion, my most beloved
Santa Muerte, my cherished Holy Death.

(Make your request here; speak with much faith.)

Simple Prayer for Money

Light a candle.

Dear Death of my heart, do not abandon me,

Proffer me your protection, both day and night.

O, my Lady, I ask you that you open the paths to success, prosperity,
and fortune, that all my requests reach you through this
blessed flame.

Thank you, my Lady, for having listened to me (make your request).

Amen.

(Recite three Our Fathers and three Hail Marys.)

So That Debtors Pay Up

Lady of my heart, do not abandon me,
With your protection and with the infinite faith, I ask that you
  be with me,
And do not give a moment's peace to (name of the person who
  owes you).
Harass them now, tomorrow, and constantly.
Do not give them a minute of tranquility
Until they pay up my money, immediately.
Thank you infinitely, my Lady of Death, for having listened to me.
Amen.

(As soon as you get paid, give an offering to Santísima Muerte.)

To Attract Money

Beloved Death, you know the sufferings of us who roam this earth.
You know well that we require clothing, shelter, and sustenance.
Help us so that the money necessary to get them reaches our pocket.
You who rule, imposing and powerful, beyond good and evil,
grant me your blessed favor.
Amen.

To Solve Financial Problems

Santa Muerte, you who help all those who need you,
I ask you to intercede to ward off the financial problems that afflict me.
You who are a great protector, guide me on the best way to find a
  solution to this pain.
Do not allow me to despair. Give me your help and open the paths so
  that all the good things come to me; allow prosperity to come to
  me, to share it with my family and live peacefully.
I ask you to give me the opportunity to find success and tranquility.
Amen.

To Get Out of Debt

O Santa Muerte,

Multiply my assets so that as soon as possible I can cover the debt of
(amount) that I owe (name of the person/bank to whom it is owed).

It has never been my intention to strip anyone of money that
is not mine.

Send the necessary money to me, that sudden windfalls come my way,
that water reaches my harvest from the arid roads, and that the
sun on me does shine.

Favor me with fortune, O Lady Death Divine.

I offer you (state promise), if you help me pay my debt,

And this I will not forget.

Amen.

For Financial Emergencies

I have spent sleepless nights looking for possible solutions.

I had no intention of bothering you, my Powerful Lady of Death,

but if I come to your altar it is because I must beg you for help.

It is because I have no choice but to come before your presence.

Santa Muerte, I require (necessary amount) to cover some expenses.

I do not ask for your help to deal with frivolity, waste, or vices.

I entrust myself to your infinite charity because I am in an emergency.

I need a miracle (amount of money) to be able to cover some payments.

If you grant me the favor that I come to ask for Santa Muerte, I
promise you (candle, flowers, chocolates) on your altar,

Very punctually, I will return you faith and gifts for the favor that
you grant me.

This miracle will help me to solve (problem), so I need (amount).

Have the certainty that I would not bother you if I could do this alone.

Santa Muerte, I request your help; I desperately have a very urgent
situation.

I cannot get the money that I need at this time,

To your holiness, I defer! O Powerful Benevolent Being! O
    Santísima Muerte!
Amen.

Prayer for Trouble at Work

My dear and beloved Santísima Muerte, I beg you with these words
    because I need your help.
At work I find myself going through problems that make me doubt
    my future.
I have been the prey of voracious vultures who want to see
    me go down.
I am suffering, sad, and drained; I need a job where there is no envy,
Where my skills are recognized, and I am given the chance to climb
    the ladder.
I need work to give my family the comfort they require.
I ask you to help me keep my job, and if it can't be, help me get a
    better one.
I ask you for an interview. I want to achieve my professional goals to
    feel fulfilled.
I want a better job, a better salary, and a job where my professional
    goals are not limited.
I want to improve my lot and life. That is why I come to you; your
    goodness and power are infinite.
I leave my problems in your hands. Thank you, I thank you infinitely,
    I am your faithful believer.
So be it.

Prayer to Find a Job

Blessed Santa Muerte,
You who see our daily struggles,
You know my great need to find
An honest and stable job

To support my home and my family,
With pure faith and love in my heart
For you and Almighty God.
Blessed Santa Muerte,
I beg you to grant me
The virtue of charity
To love God above all things,
With your intercession and your unlimited power
I ask you to grant me
This employment favor
(State your need to work, place you want to work)
Blessed Santa Muerte,
I beg you help me
With your blessings,
But especially with the blessings of health and work,
So that I can appear before you
To thank God for the work
That I received from your powerful hands.
Amen.

Prayers for Protection

For extra protection, wear a Santa Muerte pendant or bracelet, or carry a statuette on your person when you are not at home.

Protection Prayer

Holy Mother, I call on you today to request your help, my beautiful
Niña Blanca,
Do not leave me alone; I need your aid now, tomorrow, and always.
I need your will for life, because my life is your will.
In dark storms, where there is not one ray of sunshine,
I know that the solution always lies in your holy hands,

Precious Mother, you who always bring happiness to us, your children,
and erase our problems.
Through your divine power, I ask you here and now, my
beloved Death,
To cast your holy mantle of protection over my life and the life of
those I love.
Protect us from all evil and care for us. Include us in your vigil,
Holy Mother, repel and remove anything that comes to damage and
destroy me,
And allow me to live in peace.
Holy Death, cover us with your protection to scare away the wicked
and their works,
Keep us safe from the malicious and those of toxic will. My pure soul is
in your care,
My beloved and Holy Mother, protect me and my loved ones.
Amen.

Prayer for Protection from Danger

Before your divine presence, O most Holy Death, I invoke you so that
you come to my aid.
I ask you for help and protection because I feel vulnerable.
Santísima Muerte, my Niña Blanca, take care of me.
Protect me from envy so that it does not corrode my soul.
Protect me from hidden enemies and capricious destiny.
Take care of my body, mind, and spirit, because only by keeping myself
whole can I bring love to those around me.
Allow my mind to relax in the face of problems, destroy feelings that
hurt my soul, and remove stones that I may trip over.
I also ask you to break the blindfold that keeps me in the dark.
Most Holy and Beloved Niña Blanca, I ask for your total protection,
and for your forgiveness if I have offended someone.

O dearest Santa Muerte, cover me completely with your Holy Mantle
that I may be kept safe from harm, and not be seen by those who
would bring evil and darkness.
May only the light of your wonder shine on my path.
Amen.

Protection from Envy and Jealousy

Prior to proceeding, offer one black and one white candle.

Gentle Niña Blanca,

Today I ask you,

Give me strength against my enemies.

Take me and my loved ones

Far from these vile people.

I ask of you,

Clear all envy, evil, and jealousy away from us.

I ask you to remove all negative desires and thoughts that
surround me.

Loving Niña Blanca,

Today, I come before you,

Seeking thy sole protection from those around us

Who are envious of our blessings.

Even when I try to help them,

I feel that they are envious and that their negative feelings
might harm us.

Powerful Niña Blanca,

I beg you to be my eyes and ears,

Guard me from those who would hurt me out of spite or for money.

To you, Niña Blanca, I recite this humble prayer.

Niña Blanca, you are my courage and strength against my enemies.

Niña Blanca, you who have the power to turn away all that evil

That surrounds your faithful devotees,

I ask you, Niña Blanca, to take away these evil people.

Guard me and my loved ones from the deceivers, the liars, and
all enemies.
Keep us safe from hidden and unseen dangers.
Take hold of my hand and guide me on the path before me,
Opening every closed door, removing all barriers,
Opening up every road that leads me to good luck and good fortune,
Bringing me your holy blessings of health, work, and money,
Keeping me safe under your divine grace, always.
O Santísima Muerte, I thank thee.
Amen.

Prayer of Protection from Enemies, Evil, and Demonic Powers

Lord Jesus Christ, and Creator of heaven and earth, of everything
visible and
Invisible, our Lord, I ask your permission to invoke Santísima
Muerte for
In your mercy I trust.
Merciful Mother, free me from everything bad that surrounds me.
By your mercy,
I trust you to free me from the Devil, Lucifer, Satan, and all demons,
Evil, darkness, witches, sorcerers, bad neighbors, storms,
melancholy, and all
Envy.
If they have eyes,
Let them not see me.
If they have hands,
Let them not touch me.
If they have feet,
Let them not reach me.
If they have weapons,
Let them break,

That nothing shall harm me.
In your mercy, I trust Santísima Muerte, merciful Father,
in the name of the Father, the Son, and the Holy Spirit . . .
So be it.
Amen.

Prayer for Protection and Aid

Magnificent Holy Death,
Today I come crawling toward you
Struck like a dog by the hands of my enemies
With a broken heart, and shattered dreams,
My spirit crushed and my soul afflicted.
I beg and plead for your potent protection
From the liars, the thieves, and my enemies.
Most powerful Santa Muerte,
I humbly beg you, look at me with pity.
I beg you, look at me in this valley of tears,
Pleading your divine intercession before the throne of Almighty God.
Today, my Mother, I ask you from my heart (say what you need)
And I offer you this humble and modest candle
As I put all my trust, love, and devotion in you,
And I humbly await your blessings, miracles, and wonders.
Amen.

Prayer for Protection during Travel

To carry out this prayer, you will need two candles, one yellow and one red. The first should be lit one night before going on a trip; the second you will light to thank her once you have returned.

Holy Spirit of Death,
I invoke your sacred name to ask
That you help me in my travel.
Please clear my path,

On mountains, valleys, and roads.
Please offer your good fortune,
Weave destinies in such a way
That every night and every day
Malevolent wrongdoers fade before me
And that by your powerful protection I am cloaked constantly.
Please, Santa Muerte,
Ensure that no problems should show,
Or if they do, that they are resolved rapidly
And do not grow
And that they will not drown my heart.
Please ensure, dear Lady,
That no sickness take wing
Nor pain my body wrack,
Remove from my path tragedy, suffering, and lack.
This candle I light
In honor of your majesty
So that the glimmer in your eyes
Forms an invisible protective wall around me.
Give me prudence and patience.
Give me, Holy Queen of Darkness,
Strength, power, and wisdom.
With your scythe, push away the elements
So that they do not unleash their fury on me.
No matter where my path may be,
Take care of my happy return,
That I already may celebrate
And your home decorate
And a candle for you burn
On my Holy Altar
To you, my dearest Santa Muerte.
Amen.

Prayer for Protection from a Bad Neighbor

O Powerful Santa Muerte,

Rid me of terror, fear, witchcraft, sorcery, and the power of all
*   evil spells,*

And keep me from evil neighbors that seek to do me harm.

And if they look at me with an evil eye,

Protect me below your Holy Mantle of invisibility,

So that their envy cannot reach us, nor hurt my family nor me.

You who have the power to keep away all evil and conjury,

Keep away (name of bad neighbor),

Keep them busy with other things besides me.

Make it so that they have no time

To mess with my home, me, and mine.

Amen.

Prayers for Children

Protection Prayer for Children and Grandchildren

Loving Niña Blanca,

My children and my grandchildren are the true blessings of almighty
*   God in my life.*

Today I come before you to seek your total protection and your blessings,

O most Powerful Lady.

I ask you to take care of, to bless and protect my children and
*   grandchildren, whether they are asleep or awake. Watch them*
*   always with your vigilant eyes, dear Mother.*

Protect them on their way to school, while they are at school, and on
*   their way home from school.*

Protect them from other children who may wish to harm them, from
*   thugs, and wrong-doers.*

Protect them when playing outside and also in the house.

Protect them from hidden dangers, from peer pressure, and from those
    who try to adversely influence my children and grandchildren.

Defend and protect my children and grandchildren from predators
    and evil strangers and those people who wish to hurt them
    and do evil.

With your powerful hands, guide them through every step they take in
    life; keep them safe along their way.

O Niña Blanca, I ask you to use your scythe to protect them and your
    holy mantle to form a shield of total invisible protection.

Keep my children and grandchildren near you and repel storms,
    thunder, and lightning.

Protect them from hidden strangers and dangers and from sickness.
    Should they fall ill, heal them and let them recover quickly.

Please protect my children and grandchildren until the end of
    their lives.

Amen.

Prayer to Protect Children

Do not forget, Holy Lady of Death, that you too were once a child,
    small and mild.

So please protect those children that are mine, using your power holy
    and divine.

I ask you, loving Lady, take care of (names of the children).

Please ensure that nothing bad happens to my children, use your hand
    and scythe to keep away danger, evil, and the malevolent stranger.

Take care of their health and help them to be good people; make
    their hearts innocent and pure; keep them prudent, determined,
    forevermore.

Make them work hard and be good throughout their entire childhood.
    Do not let others lead them astray, and please watch over them
    each and every night and day.

Amen.

Women's Prayer

Santa Muerte,
I, your fervent servant, ask you for me
And all those women who work hard daily
To bring home the daily bread,
That we do not lack prosperity,
That the doors to success be wide open constantly.
I also ask for those who study,
To help them meet their goals successfully.
Protect our paths, every night and day.
May we always be respected as daughters, mothers, grandmothers,
    lovers, wives.
All evil and danger around us, please sweep away.
Use your scythe to remove every man who wants to hurt, harm
    us, or abuse.
Bless our marriage or dating so that love is never missing in our lives.
Santa Muerte, whatever problem I have I trust in you,
And I know you will not leave me alone, so please help me (make
    your request).
I am a woman, I am your devotee,
And I will be until the last day of my life, faithfully,
My life is in your hands, and I will walk calmly as I understand
And know you are with me and you will not leave me alone.
Bless and protect my friends and my family.
Keep away all falsehood, hurt, evil, and hypocrisy.
I thank you, I know you listen to me.
You give me much wisdom, patience, and the sobriety
To walk with my head held high and calmly in this society.
I ask nothing but respect,
Because I am a woman,
And have the same rights as anybody.
You are fair, and you will not allow me to suffer any shame.

Secrets of Santa Muerte

I am a woman, I am your devotee and worship your name,
I will be until the last day of my life,
And my requests will be heard.
Amen.

Prayer for Pregnancy

O Santa Muerte, Beloved Mother,
You who have the power of life and death in your hands.
Today I come to ask you to grant me what I long for.
I ask you, most Blessed Death,
That you see the pain that my heart is suffering
Not being able to carry the fruit of love in my womb.
That is why I turn to you, Holy Holy Death.
To pray to you, Santa Muerte, to get pregnant.
Because I don't know what else to do, and I feel so overwhelmed.
As yours is death and life,
I ask you to kill this great pain that is in my heart,
And bring life to my womb and peace to my heart.
I promise, my dearest Saint, that if you grant my wish,
I will worship and venerate you for the rest of my days.
I also promise you, to instill your values in the fruit of my womb
So that I too am loving and adoring just like you, my Mother.
So that my child too loves you as I do.
Today I ask you, Holy Mother, that you put yourself in my body,
That you cleanse my insides, and once cleansed, gift me life
     within my womb,
Because if I can't be a mother, I don't want to continue.
But if you grant me my prayer and my wish is fulfilled,
O Santa Muerte
I promise to be faithful to you, and always to worship you forevermore,
until the day you decide to take me with you.
Amen

Prayers for the Family

Prayer for Family Well-Being

Blessed Most Holy Death,
With all my heart, I thank you for your blessings and your protection
over my family.
Blessed dearest Santa Muerte,
I pray that you help us to unite as a family.
Blessed Most Holy Death,
I humbly ask you to help us to speak calmly
So that my family members do not fight among themselves.
Blessed dearest Santa Muerte
I pray that you guide us and keep us on the right track.
I pray that gossip, rumors, or lies against my family do not thrive.
Blessed Most Holy Death,
I beg you to protect my home and my family from crime,
harm, and evil.
I also pray that should harm come toward us
That it befalls my enemy's family, not mine,
And that it divide our enemies and never cause dissension
in our home.
Blessed Most Holy Death,
I pray that you will help us stay united,
preferring to be with each other over outsiders,
And that we stay together as a family with tight bonds
Loving above all else each other.
Blessed Beloved Santa Muerte,
I ask this in the name of Jesus.
Amen.

Prayer for Solving Family Issues

With sadness nailed to my soul, yet great hope,
I ask that you intercede for me on this desperate day.
Today I come to implore you, pure Santa Muerte,
that you remove with your Grace, all our bitterness!
Disputes and altercations stain the peace of my family! They argue and
    quarrel for no reason! So to you I come to speak, Santa Muerte,
    in this prayer, to ask that you protect my family and bring
    them calm.
I know that you would never deny me, what I ask of you here, O, Holy
    and Glorious Death! Turn this strong storm into a gentle breeze
    and a bed of roses.
Preserve the family love that I love so much! And bring back the
    happiness for which I have always fought! Bring back the love,
    unity, and beauty that previously existed in this home!
Today is an ordeal, O, sincere and loving Mother; please save me from
    this sordid environment of screams and pain! End these conflicts
    that damage family peace, and help me in this harsh moment,
    Celestial Lady!
Let no one else express their resentment, hatred, and ignorance with
    hurtful words! Quiet their hatred and pettiness!
I ask you not to ignore me, Lady of the White Veils! This is my request!
    (Make your request.) Do what you can and please hear my
    cry of help!
I'll make it up to you with (offer your reward, in return).
    Unconditionally, I shall be your servant and you will be praised
    and revered!
I know that you are able to grant me everything I ask of you and much
    more, blessed Santa Muerte!
Thank you for always listening to me and bringing me comfort.
I worship you always.
Amen.

Prayer to Protect Your Family

I have come to pray to you, Holy Lady, with my most
fervent devotion!

There are warnings in my dreams, and concerns in my soul, that I
must take care of forever!

Thank you for listening to me, with your Sacred Goodness, Pretty
Lady, you who illuminate and ignite the mysteries of prayers and
faith, of all those who pray to you!

Cover with your mantle, my children, Santa Muerte; let no one stand
between them and their luck! Let no one hurt my brothers, sisters,
parents, and grandparents (change according to family members),
let them have perfect health and a long life!

O, Most Holy Death, I beg you, do not abandon my husband/wife;
guide them on their path so that vices and women/men do not
come into their life! Let your power protect him/her against
hidden grudges and malice!

O, Lady of Mysteries who brings us to the Hereafter! I know that you
are transcendent in your Immortal mission! Next to God himself,
you have learned to be Holy, the purest and most Heavenly!

May your Omnipotence unite us in life! Let us all be together, side
by side! Let us be a family full of health, happiness, and of
abundance! I ask you for them, for my family (make your request),
grant me your Grace, please!

Let us be a family that loves and respects each other, O, my Holy
Girl, you cannot fail me! I promise you that your Grace will be
rewarded! (Make your offering.)

I place my prayer before your image, full of dreams and good energy!
I present my wish to your noble soul! And let it fly! O, Virtuous
Saint, who are here before me on your Altar! Beloved Death of
My Heart! Let it be so!

Amen.

Prayer for Justice

Blessed Santa Muerte,

Protector of the weak and helpless.

Mother of eternal justice,

Mistress of wisdom,

You who look into the hearts of the good and the bad,

I approach you, Lady, to implore you for justice.

To you, Santísima Muerte,

I request the impartiality of your scales.

(State your petition.)

My Lady, see my heart,

Listen to my prayers, that come out of need,

Please may justice be done on this Earth,

May your divine hand guide the decisions of judges and jailors.

Powerful Lady,

Be ruthless with the wicked and backstabbers.

Be fair with the innocent,

And benevolent with those who repent

Of heart and spirit.

O Santa Muerte,

Hear my prayers and protect me

From indolence and iniquity.

On this day I request your favor in this supplication

That my case be submitted for your consideration

And that I obtain absolute forgiveness

Of all the earthly judges.

When the time comes, you will judge me,

And you will take the words that I have now pledged

As the measure of my punishment or my absolution.

Amen.

Prayer for Justice 2

Blessed Most Holy Death,
Guardian of the fragile, the wronged, and the innocent,
Lady of Supreme Intelligence,
You, for who no matter if she/he is good or bad,
Piously watch over their heart,
I come before you today, Lady,
To beg you for jurisprudence.
To you, Santa Muerte, I turn
For the impartiality of your scales of justice.
Lady of the Night,
Look inside my heart.
Set your gaze on my pleas which cause me to cry out.
Let the earth feel your righteous scythe,
May it be your sacred hand that points the way to
The decisions made by judges upon prisoners.
Good Lady,
Be harsh with the guilty
And those who deserve it,
Be sweet with the uncorrupted and with the innocent,
And forgive those of us who regret our deeds and repent
If it is truly, of soul, heart, and mind.
O, Santa Muerte!
Heed my prayers
And shelter me from all infamy
And indolence, and anything that may threaten me.
Today, I ask for your attention
So that in my judgment you are the one who directs all,
And that your decision guides the judges who will decide my fate.
Let them feel my injustice and let me be pardoned,
Do not let me fall.
When it's my time, you will be the one to judge me,

and you will judge me by my testimony,
That I now offer to you as a gift,
and you will decide whether I am to be delivered from judgment
or if not, determine my punishment.
Amen.

Prayer against Robbery

I ask for your protection, Santa Muerte.
Keep thieves away from these doors,
Cover intruders with your white cloak
So that they do not rob.
Take care of my assets at all moments.
Guard ceilings and walls from evil intentions.
Do not allow lost spirits
To lead their followers here.
Save my home, my business from all evil,
I toss these coins before you
To show that above all material things you are the most important.
(Offer nine coins to Santa Muerte and leave them before her.)
With you by my side, I will no longer be afraid.
So be it.
Amen.

Prayer for Justice in the Face of Betrayal

Great Death, both fierce and compassionate,
Listen to the voice of this soul that calls you,
I kneel before your imposing presence,
To ask you to remove from me the anger that destroys and
    embitters all.
Santísima Muerte, ruthless yet considerate,
Take care of me and with your hand, expel me from the venomous
    anger and wrath that knows no patience.

Santísima Muerte, Lady of the Night, Lady of Destinies,

On this day I approach you to ask, beg you, to hear my complaint
against (person's name).

This person (explain situation).

Mother of mine, use your righteous hand as for you there is nothing
impossible,

That is why I ask you with your power to not let (person's name) get
away with their actions,

For they have deceived and betrayed me.

My Mother, if it were not a difficult situation, I would not dare to ask
for your help. But you know of my need, of my despair. I trust in
you to bring justice to (person's name), so that traitors and liars,
those with a silver tongue, do not go unpunished.

Lady of the Night, may your scythe fall relentlessly on the liar and
deceiver (person's name). Because you have dominion over life
and death, give (person's name) no quarter, neither in body nor in
spirit until there is justice in my case.

So be it.

Amen.

Prisoner's Prayer

Beloved brother, you were born free, your all-powerful spirit is free,
although your physical body is not.

The presence of death is within me (your name).

She always accompanies me.

I want to confess that I really am very sorry for the sin that led me to
this situation.

I invoke the presence of Holy Death to set me free,

To live in liberty as is the right of every living being.

Amen!

Prayers for Hexing, Cursing, and Keeping Enemies at Bay

Death to My Enemies

Two black candles and incense or tobacco are needed for this prayer.

Peace is achieved only through the shedding of the first blood,
As you know,
O Santa Muerte,
Eternal Lady with a cosmic cloak
Who roams free on this earth,
With the Scented breath of wilted flowers which intoxicate
     your essence,
With your Powerful shield that protects those who know and exalt
     your name,
With your potent infinite spirit that rotates without rest,
You who are the battering ram of the divine,
You who turn what is finite into eternity,
O stealthy shadow that travels into the deepest abyss of the underworld
With the relentless edge of your scythe stained with scarlet
You who cut everything that binds us.
Before the flame of these two black candles, I invoke your presence.
Through this offering of fire and smoke, I nourish your essence
For your colossal power to manifest within me
And make me one with your spiritual shadow.
In this night of no return, I invoke the powers of your scythe
So that its edge spills the blood of my enemy.
In this restless night
I beg for the intervention of anger silenced by eons of private torment.
Whisper in my ear the names of my known and hidden enemies.
Before the cock crows, my enemies will know the strength of
     your hand,

And they will feel cold shivers running through their skin when your
shadow rises.
Before sunset,
Their contempt and resentment for me will have turned to terror,
And then they will know that there will be no corner on earth where
they can hide their flesh.
O mighty Santa Muerte, yours is my plea
And mine is your strength to face everything that limits me.
May your protective scythe spill the blood of my enemies
And tear down every wall that rises in my path
I forever entrust my flesh to your force,
And I entrust eternally my soul to your shadowy spirit.
Always guide me on my path,
Show me how I may always know you and show you deepest devotion,
Going above and beyond my mortal senses.
O Santa Muerte (Repeat seven times)

Prayer to the Seven Powers of Santa Muerte to Destroy an Enemy

Blessed Santa Muerte,
You who see everything and hear everything,
You know the evils that my enemies have done to me.
That's why I invoke you at this moment to listen to my request:
O glorious Niña Blanca, I ask that
You end the life of (person's name).
I ask you to bring prompt destruction to their life.
O virtuous Niña Dorada, I ask you to
Cut off all their money and destroy the business of (enemy's name).
O Dearest Niña Roja, I ask you to
End all their relationships and cut love from their life of
(person's name).
O wondrous Santa Muerte Azul,

I ask you to remove all peace, tranquility, and friendship
From the life of (person's name).
Make them mad, and make them mistrust all company.
O Niña Verde, I ask you
To plague them with legal problems
And to make justice turn against (person's name).
O Amber Santa Muerte,
I ask that you bring terrible vices and misfortunes to (person's name).
Make them lose control of their life right now.
O Beautiful Niña Negra,
I ask you to bring misfortune, disease, and death to (person's name).
Make their life be full of danger, dread, and misery.
Let it be so.
Amen.

Hexing of Enemies and Prayer for Personal Protection

Three black candles are needed for this prayer and an offering of incense.

O Santísima Muerte, protect me in every step I take.
Most Holy Death, cover me with your sacred mantle from all danger.
Let your powerful shadow always advance in front of me, behind me,
    to my left, and to my right to protect me.
Let your fist punch powerfully all those who want to see me destroyed.
Let your scythe slash every attempt by my enemies to destroy me.
Let your scythe cut every obstacle that is forced upon me.
Let your footprints trace the path that my feet have to follow and
    through which I will find the liberation of my soul at the end of
    this journey.
Santísima Muerte,
Raise your powerful hand against all my enemies,
Slice away all the negative energy that they seek to use against me.
Make them aware of your power and strength.
Rid them from my life forever and guide them to your deadly path.

Nothing and nobody can escape your presence,
Manifest yourself in their nights,
And make them understand that you are my guardian and my
    protector.
Cloud their sight so they can no longer see me.
Close their mouth so they can't talk about me.
Cover their ears so they can't hear me.
Tie their hands and feet so they can't reach nor touch me.
And don't let them rest
Until all those bad thoughts of me are out of their minds.
Make them feel your presence until they completely forget about me.
Santísima Muerte, my Mighty Queen,
I offer you these three black candles and the smoke of this incense to
    seal our pact,
Accept my offering and nourish yourself with its essence.
So be it!
Amen.

Prayer to Destroy Any Enemy

Santísima Muerte,
Queen of Destruction,
You who are both my boss and my guide,
With this prayer I beg and plead you
To destroy any enemy who wishes to harm me.
I trust in your steady scythe that you will aid me
To end all evil,
To cut all envy,
And that I will live safely
Under your guidance forever.
Amen.

Prayer of Victory over My Enemy

O Holy Lady, Santa Muerte,
You, the ultimate conqueror,
Who have the powers to work miracles,
Who have scourged the dead with thorns and buried them,
You who have triumphed over all
And crushed your enemies and buried them in hell,
I praise and bless your holy name
And I ask you, O Lady, O Santa Muerte,
Grant me the graces of being the victor of my enemies (name them).
Let me be vanquished, not persecuted, and set me free from all
    enemies, Santa Muerte.
Amen.

Prayer of Revenge

O Holy and Divine Death,
you who observe all humans and
You who know how much I have suffered,
I ask you to do justice for me.
May you strike a blow on the one who did me wrong (name them).
Make them pay for all the damage they have done to me.
Blessed Santa Muerte, take revenge for me,
No matter what the price, give them what they deserve.
So be it.
Amen.

Prayer to Invoke Most Holy Death against Any Enemy

Lady Death,
Skeletal Spirit, most powerful and strong,
You who are unbeatable in the moment of danger,
I invoke you humbly for your blessings.
I pray, almighty Santa Muerte, that you grant me

Everything I ask of you.
Let the one who hurt me or cast upon me an evil eye
Turn away from me right now
And repent their actions for their whole life.
For the one who deceives me in love,
I ask that you bring this love back to me,
And if they ignore your strange voice,
Good Spirit of Death,
Make them feel the power of your scythe.
In business, justice, and the game of life
I name you my lawyer,
And if anyone should take steps to hurt me
Or go against me,
Make them the loser in this life.
O Lady Death, my protective angel.
Amen.

Prayer for Protection from Enemies

Most Virtuous Lady,
Guardian of the world,
I ask you for your love
And that of Our Lord Jesus Christ,
May you free me from the constant attacks
Of my enemies.
Let them not be cruel to me,
Save me from sudden death
From nosy neighbors.
And if I go to jail, console me
And free me with honor
And the power of Death on high.
From envious people
And malicious enemies,

Cover me with your mantle.
And cut them with your scythe.
I humbly ask you,
Santa Muerte.
Amen.

Prayers against Gossip and Envy

Prayer against Evil and Gossip

Santísima Muerte, help me with your miracles; I believe in your
justice because I have faith in God,
Our Father,
That is why I ask you to remove from my path and stop the loose
tongue of (person's name).
They are bothering me, O Lady of Death,
I ask that they forget about me and that you use your glorious
intercession to let me live in peace.
Beloved counselor of Death, spread your mantle of power over me so
that evil does not come to me.
Should my enemy shoot poison looks at me,
Let these never come to hurt me and let evil turn into good.
In the name of the Father, the Son, and the Holy Spirit, thank you for
listening to me, Most Holy Death.
So be it.
Amen.

Prayer against Gossip and Slander for Yourself and Family

In the name of almighty Jesus,
And under the cloak of your protection,
I (name of person praying),
At this moment ask you to seal the lips of every person

Of every man or woman who seeks to tarnish my name, or that of
    my family,
Especially from (person's name).
Seal their lips; close them forever.
Let no word come out that disturbs my existence,
Tie any tongue that speaks ill of me,
Silence the mouths of all wicked people.
I ask almighty God for his protection.
And may you, Santa Muerte, judge them relentlessly.
Those who seek to harm me,
Wherever they go, may they be rejected by their own hatred.
Wherever they go, may the doors be closed.
May they not get a moment's peace at night when they sleep.
May their souls have no rest for blaspheming.
Let them seek repentance for causing me so much pain,
And, Santa Muerte, unleash all your power against them
Because they have caused pain in my soul.
I ask you from my heart, Santa Muerte, full of justice,
You who hates gossip and blasphemy.
Amen.

Prayer for Ending Gossip and Envy

Blessed Santa Muerte,
Give me strength against my enemies,
And today I ask you
That you remove all envy directed at me,
All gossip and evil.
That all the negative wishes
Of those around me
Return to their owner.
Santísima Muerte,
Let your eyes be my eyes

And may your punishment fall upon those
Who wish to do me evil out of envy
Or for money seek to hurt me.
In your hands,
I leave the punishment and price of their actions.
Blessed Santa Muerte,
Build me a spiritual fortress against my enemies.
I entrust myself to your hands.
Amen.

Sicario Prayer

If they have eyes,
Let them not see me.
If they have hands,
Let them not touch me.
If they have feet
Let them not reach me.
Let them not surprise me from behind.
Let them not spill my blood.
May my death not be violent.
You who know everything,
You who know of my sins,
But also know of my faith,
Never abandon me, O Santa Muerte.
Amen.

Tapa Boca Prayer (Shut up!)

O, Most Holy and Powerful Lady of the Night!
I ask that you judge and use your cosmic sight
To punish the one that sought to harm me and criticize
With nasty talk, gossip, and lies.
Shut their mouth and seal it tight.

Cover up and close their eyes;
Block and bind their ears,
And may all their senses disappear.
So that person and anyone else
Who seeks to bother me with their bad tongue,
Be silenced and rendered deaf and dumb.
Let all evil they send me be returned threefold.
Blessed be, my Queen of Darkness and Cold.
Amen.

CHAPTER SEVEN

Spells:
Hechizos and *Brujeria*

Please remember to work with the moon phases when you work *brujeria*. For all benevolent magic, it is vital to work on a clean altar with a cleansed soul and mind that is not sullied by other energies and to work with focus. While the incantations in this book offer important instructions and provide vital magical foundations for you to work within, in Santa Muerte, the successful *bruja* or *brujo* brings a personal touch to their *brujeria*, and so should you. They infuse it with the power of their intent and, through a deep bond with Santa Muerte, imbue their *hechizos* (spells) with Death's touch. This skill cannot be taught through any book, and only you alone can learn to master this through deep devotion and flowing into Santa's sacred realm. You should also learn to improvise. If an ingredient is not available to you, feel free to substitute it with what your intuition and Santa Muerte guide you to replace it with; of course, this must be appropriate to your intentions, the situation, and the outcome you desire. If you feel that additional details are needed to ensure the spell outlines your exact objectives, you may wish to add your own words to conjurations. While you should work within the frameworks provided, with appropriate ingredients, magic is achieved not by following verbatim every instruction within this chapter, but rather by creating a sacred space within which you direct energies, using your own intention, intuition, and above all, kindling magic through your personal connection to Santa Muerte, fusing with her power of life and death.

Love Spells

Simple Love Spell

This spell is very simple to do and its effectiveness is said to be high.

Ingredients:

sheet of paper
pen
2 red Santa Muerte candles
1 red Santa Muerte statue
red rose
red apple
red candy

Take the sheet of paper and write a letter to Santa Muerte asking what you want from your partner, either to come to you, return, or be faithful to you. Explain what you want to transpire with your partner.

Light the two red candles and place them in front of the red Santa Muerte statue. In the middle of the two red candles, place your letter; on the letter, place the rose. Offer Santa Muerte the red apple and the candy.

Let the candles burn completely without putting them out. Then fold the letter with the rose in the middle, and keep it hidden under your pillow for nine days. After that, keep it in your bedroom somewhere close by, but hidden.

In nine days, you will see the changes that you asked for in your partner.

Love Spell to Draw Your Loved One to You

Ingredients:

9 photos of a loved one

pen

red Santa Muerte candle

rose oil

cinnamon oil

coyote oil (if you can find it)

image of la Niña Roja

matches

12 red roses

offerings of apples, cinnamon, and honey

rosary

(Make sure you also have fresh water and alcoholic libations.)

Before starting to prepare the entire spell, note that this ritual must be performed for nine days between 10 p.m. and 11 p.m. It is vital to start on the first day of the week: on Monday.

In each of the nine photos, you must write the love wish that you want to be fulfilled by Santa Muerte.

On the first day anoint your candle with rose, cinnamon, and coyote oil. Rest against it the printed image of Santa Muerte; then light your red candle in front of the statue of Santa Muerte and place the nine photos around it in a circle. Burn rose incense and waft it over the photos and over Santa Muerte and yourself. Give her the offerings of roses, apples, cinnamon, and honey.

Recite the following:

> *O Santa Muerte,*
> *You who listen to the faithful devotee,*
> *I come begging to your deathly door,*
> *Please grant me your gifts*
> *And with your magical majesty*
> *Attract to my side forevermore*
> *This soul (person's name),*
> *That you now bind,*
> *To me (your name,) and all that is mine.*
> *Please grant this to me,*

> *O Protector of Death,*
> *Santa Muerte of my heart, soul, and body*
> *And in debt to you I will remain infinitely.*
> *Amen.*

After reciting this verse, place the rosary around the neck of Santa Muerte and do not remove it until the ninth day.

When this is done, state very clearly the exact love favor to Santa Muerte, clearly expressing what you want in this new relationship. Then burn the first photo and keep the ashes in a pot on the altar.

Leave the candle burning for nine minutes; then extinguish it by tapping it with a spoon or other object.

The next day, perform the same ritual again, wafting incense and refreshing offerings as needed. From here on, the petition changes to

> *O Santa Muerte,*
> *I am your son/daughter.*
> *I gladly come to fulfill my offerings before you,*
> *and to ask,*
> *bring (person's name) to my side*
> *and my debt to you will be vast.*
> *Amen.*

Again, leave the candle burning for nine minutes, then extinguish it by tapping it with a spoon or other object. Also burn the image of the loved one and keep the ashes in the pot.

Do this daily for nine days with all the photos until they have all been burnt. To complete the love spell, on the ninth day, recite and follow these instructions:

> *Today my great sacrifice ends,*
> *O, Mother of Death,*
> *Do not let my prayers*
> *Leave me bereft.*

On this day, after completely burning the last image, add the ashes to the others.

Leave the candle burning until it is completely consumed. Do not put it out, even when you are sleeping.

After this, cast the ashes to the wind. An especially good location is one where you met or have passed pleasant moments with your loved one. Make more offerings to Holy Death. Carry the printed image of red Santa Muerte on you—for example, in your wallet or bag. When your petition comes through, buy Santa Muerte red roses and other gifts.

The *curandera* who gifted me this spell told me:

•••••✳•••••

It is important to note that this love binding can be very power-ful, so it is recommended to use it only when you are fully con-vinced that the person chosen is the one for life. Although its effectiveness begins on day four or five, it is almost guaranteed that the person you love will sooner or later fall into your arms.

•••••✳•••••

It should be noted that love spells with Santa Muerte may carry a cost for those who perform them, so do not be surprised if she takes something else from you or tests you in exchange for the love of your life. This red magic spell pushes the envelope. Use it at your own risk.

Red Ribbon Love Spell

This spell is to ensure your partner keeps loving you.

Ingredients:

red candle
red Santa Muerte statue
rose incense
rose oil or rose water
honey
red roses

red ribbon
black pen

First, light a red candle and place your red Santa Muerte statue next to it. Cover them both with rose incense, and waft this over yourself. Anoint yourself and your Santa Muerte statue with rose oil or rose water. Give Most Holy Death offerings of honey and red roses. After doing this, on a red ribbon, using a black pen, write your name and your beloved's name. After this, write this message:

> *Niña Roja, Santa Muerte, I beg you to use your scythe to cut any kind of evil working against this love relationship that I have. May love never be lacking and may happiness shine at all times in our relationship and may everything flow with love until our last days, when we are together. Amen!*

Then tie the ribbon on the candle. Dab it lightly with rose oil or rose water. After doing this, choose one of the prayers of love from chapter six, depending on your needs; then pray to Santa Muerte every morning and night for nine days in a row. You must pray at the following times: 11:11 a.m. and 11:11 p.m.

The witch who gave me this spell told me:

···❋···❋···❋···❋···❋···❋···❋···❋···

This type of love binding with Santa Muerte can be commenced on any day of the week, but it is said that it will be strongest and have its most powerful effect if done on a special day for your couple, such as your wedding anniversary or Valentine's day or another day that is meaningful to you and your loved one. On such days, energy radiates from your being with more intensity, and love beats very strong. If the saint decides that she or he is the right person for you, everything will be done as you wish it.

···❋···❋···❋···❋···❋···❋···❋···❋···

Love Spell for Total Fidelity

This spell, from a witch in Chimalhuacan, is not for the faint of heart. It demands a lot of candles, which can be plain wax tapers, and a lot of time, as well as a visit to a graveyard. But it is absolutely binding, so I am told. If you are doing it for someone else, such as a couple you know, put a photo of the couple in the coconut, or two photos that you place with faces facing each other and rolled up as one.

Ingredients:

coconut
cloves
rose oil
Pajaro macuo oil (optional)
rose petals
rose water
21 red candles, 21 purple candles, 21 pink candles
photograph of the person you love
honey
small rose-flavored piece of candy
cork
bar of pure chocolate
red Statue of Santa Muerte

Make a hole in the coconut so you can insert elements into it, but do not make it too big.

Remove the coconut water and mix it with a few cloves, nine drops of rose oil, three drops of *pajaro macua* oil (optional), rose petals, and rose water. Then add this mixture to some warm water. Bathe in it to do a limpia of love.

On every single candle, write the name of the person whose fidelity you seek.

Write the name of the person on the back of the photo, and write "Santa Muerte, Come to Me."

Roll up the photo and insert it in the coconut through the small hole. Also insert honey, rose petals, and the small, rose-flavored piece of candy.

Seal the coconut with the piece of cork, and then melt the chocolate and pour it over the coconut and all over the shell, sealing it totally in its sweetness,

Light the candles, three at a time in front of Santa Muerte—that is to say, one red, one pink, one purple. Place them in a straight line in front of la Niña Roja and let them burn constantly.

Over twenty days, you will light three new candles each night, placing them in the same position.

On the twenty-first day, make your petition to Santa Muerte, pray to her fervently, and say the rosary (see chapter six).

When all the candles have burnt, take the coconut and go to the graveyard. Dig a hole and bury it there with whatever remains of the candles.

Spell for Sexual Fidelity and Never-Ending Lust and Love

This spell is to make someone crave your body day and night and be yours in body and mind forever.

Ingredients:

6 red Santa Muerte candles

honey

long strip of parchment paper

feather of a chicken (or other bird if unavailable)

blood of a chicken (spotted hen); you may choose to use your menstrual blood instead

clay plate

2 pubic hairs (1 from each person)

rose oil

vanilla oil

coyote oil or Doblegado a Mis Pies (on your knees) oil, which can be replaced by jasmine or cinnamon oil as necessary

1 red face-to-face lovers couple candle

Prepare the six red candles as follows: cover them on all sides with honey. Cut a long, thin strip from the parchment paper, and with the feather, using chicken or menstrual blood, write the name of the two people and say the following:

> *In the name of Santa Muerte, you who alone unite and only you who can separate, conjoin us forever till death do us part.*

Cover the clay plate with honey, and, in the very center, place the pubic hairs entwined together. On top of that, add a few drops of each essential oil on the paper and place the red couples candle right at the center of the plate. Using the long, thin strip of parchment paper, wrap it around the couple as many times as you can, binding them together with a knot to seal the spell work.

Place the entire spell work on your altar to Santa Muerte. Place three red Santa Muerte candles to the left and three to the right of the clay plate. Light all the candles from left to right, finishing by lighting the couple in the middle.

Say the following:

> *Powerful being, Strong and Mighty, O Santa Muerte, of light and love, I invoke you and ask you, Red Lady, to intercede with your divine energy, that you make manifest what I ask of you in this love spell. You who are immortality, bring to me (person's name); let them be mine eternally. Let them crave me madly, pine for me always, and love me forever until the last day, hour, and moment that your Divine Majesty orders us to be brought before your presence forever.*
>
> *I will honor your miraculous energy till the last of my days. I offer to your holy presence these essences, these candles, and my faith as well as all my prayers, O powerful, beautiful Santa Muerte. Hear me in the name of the Father, the Son, and the Holy Ghost, O Santa Muerte. Amen.*

Say this prayer every night until the candles have all finished. Then take the spellwork in a bag and leave it in the cemetery.

Spell to Forget a Lover

If you have been let down in love and keep thinking of the person, this spell will allow you to let go of that person forever and move on.

Ingredients:

piece of brown paper: 10 × 10 cm
small red or pink Santa Muerte statue
hemp twine: 2 yards
clay jug
chamomile essential oil
aloe vera
soothing balsam (balsamo tranquilo)
foil: 20 × 20 cm
2 white Santa Muerte candles

Write the name of the lover you want to forget on the brown paper. Place the small Santa Muerte statue on the brown paper and wrap that up to make a package. Use the hemp twine to seal the package completely. Put the package in the clay jug. Then gently pour the essential oil into the jug and squeeze some aloe vera into it. After this, pour the balsam into the jug. Close the jug completely by using the foil to create a lid that covers it. Now recite the following:

> *Please attend to my petition,*
> *Santa Muerte,*
> *O Great Lady,*
> *I am your faithful devotee.*
> *Please let me forget (person's name) totally.*
> *Make it so I will never again think of their love, caresses, nor*
>   *affection.*
> *And remove from me any desire for (person's name) and any*
>   *connection.*
> *So be it and so let it be.*

Put the jug on your altar. Light the candles and keep them lit until they burn completely.

After they have burnt, throw away the jug or bury it in some large bushes. When you throw it out, all love you have for the person will vanish forever.

Spells for Money

Spell for Easy Money

This ritual to Santa Muerte for easy money is very effective. Ask Santa Muerte to help you attract money and luck to your life. I was told this ritual should be done on a Monday at 7:00 a.m. or 7:00 p.m., to ensure its effect. Swap the gold candle for a yellow if it is luck over finances that are needed.

Ingredients:

paper and pencil
honey
statue of Santa Muerte (ideally gold, yellow, or siete potencias)
1 gold or yellow Santa Muerte candle
7 coins
7 bay leaves
small earthenware plate

To begin, take the paper and write the name of the person to whom this ritual is dedicated. If it is yourself, write your name. Then take a little honey and cover the candle with it. Now go to your altar and place the candle in front of your Santa Muerte statue, light the golden candle, and place the seven coins around it.

Repeat this phrase seven times:

> *O blessed and beloved Santa Muerte, I decree that today the doors of fortune and prosperity will open to me.*

Then write one of the following words on each of the bay leaves:

On the first, write MONEY.

On the second, write LUCK.

On the third, write PROSPERITY.

On the fourth, write ABUNDANCE.

On the fifth, write GOOD OPPORTUNITIES.

On the sixth, write WEALTH.

On the seventh, write SUCCESS.

Recite the following:

> *Blessed and powerful Santa Muerte, I humbly come to ask you please to open the doors of fortune and prosperity for (say your name, or that of the person to whom you dedicate the ritual). I promise to (make a promise to Santa Muerte of a gift, etc.) when you come through for me.*

After this, at your altar, say the following sentences with all your faith and burn each bay leaf in order, using the flame of the candle over the earthenware plate.

> *At this moment I decree that the MONEY will come and I burn the first leaf.*
> *At this moment I decree that LUCK will come and I burn the second leaf.*
> *At this moment I decree that PROSPERITY will come and I burn the third leaf.*
> *At this moment I decree that ABUNDANCE will come and I burn the fourth leaf.*
> *At this time I decree that GOOD OPPORTUNITIES will come and I burn the fifth leaf.*

> *At this moment I decree that WEALTH will come and I burn the*
> *sixth leaf.*
> *At this moment I decree that SUCCESS will come and I burn the*
> *seventh leaf.*

Now let the candle burn out completely. Once this is done, gather the burnt bay leaves, the candle, and coins. Leave them in a beautiful, sunny place that feels positive and is close to your home, work, or other place where money may come to you. Thank Santa Muerte for listening.

Spell for Abundance and Money

Ingredients:

new white porcelain plate

3 green Santa Muerte candles; if Santa Muerte candles are not available,
use tapers instead in this spell

3 yellow Santa Muerte candles

3 gold Santa Muerte candles

3 silver Santa Muerte candles

1 white Santa Muerte candle

13 kernels of white corn

13 black corn kernels

13 yellow corn kernels

100% pure and natural gold dust

13 coins of different denominations

1 pure cigar

On a new, white porcelain plate on your altar, arrange the thirteen candles, scatter the corn, the gold powder, and the coins, invoking Santa Muerte. Blow smoke over her as you recite:

> *Ven Ven Dinero, Come Money*
> *Money, come come come.*
> *I have great faith*
> *For the money will come*

And won't go away.
This much I want it, so let it be so.
Santa Muerte, I greet you,
I worship you.
Give me good luck
Happiness, love, health,
And a lot of money.
Money, come come come,
You will always accompany me
As a good friend you are.
Money, come come come,
I need you not to stray too far.
You will arrive by all means
And you will be my great friend for life.
Money, COME COME COME!

Do this every day for nine days in a row.

Spell to Secure a Job

Unlike with most spells, you should do this one in bright sun, preferably at noon if you can. If you can't find all three types of incense, stick with patchouli.

Ingredients:

big white plate
3 coins
3 candles in green, yellow, and gold
image of Santa Muerte or small gold Santa Muerte statue
piece of whole orris root (raiz de lirio); powder also will work
3 sticks of incense in laurel, bergamot, and patchouli

Set up your plate, and place three coins in a triangle. Place each candle on a coin and light it. Place the statue of Santa Muerte and the orris root piece in the center between the three candles.

If you can't find all three types of incense, you can replace them with frankincense, myrrh, or other money-attracting incenses such as *lluvia de dinero* (let it rain money) incense, but they should be of three different types.

Recite the following:

> *Niña Dorada, I'm ready and waiting. (Light the laurel incense.)*
> *Niña Dorada, I'm right for this job. (Then light the*
> *bergamot incense.)*
> *Niña Dorada, I'm waiting for your call. (Then light the patchouli*
> *incense.)*

Let the smoke from the incense build up on top of your candles, and focus on what your life would be like if you got this job. Keep everything lit until the candles and incense are finished. Take the piece of orris root and the image/statue of the Santa Muerte and keep it in your pocket until you get the job. If you cannot find the root, you may use powder, placing it in a cotton pouch or other soft receptacle with the statue, so that you can carry it in your pocket easily.

Spell to Improve Your Relationship with Your Boss

Ingredients:

rosemary, laurel, and chamomile herbs
large pot
water
cane sugar or honey
piece of paper
blue pen
1 blue ribbon
1 yellow ribbon
1 coconut
circassion or mustard seeds; if you are asking for a pay raise, use gold flakes
    or polvo doble suerte (double luck powder)
your perfume
1 piece of aluminum foil

1 cigar

1 piece of your clothing

*7 different colored candles representing each of Santa Muerte's powers
(white, red, black, blue, yellow, green, purple)*

Boil the rosemary, laurel, and chamomile in a large pot as you focus on improving your relationship with your boss. Sprinkle a bit of sugar or honey into it. Set a little of the elixir aside in a cup or other receptacle. Bathe in the rest of the mixture.

Dress in clean clothes, then go to your altar. Write your full name and date of birth on the piece of paper. Below that, write your boss's full name and date of birth if known. Fold the paper in half and then fold it in half again. Wrap the blue ribbon around it and then the yellow to make a package. If asking for a pay raise, consider also adding gold ribbon. As you do this, ask Santa Muerte to improve your relationship with your boss and express your needs.

Make a hole in the coconut large enough to place the package in. Pour the coconut water out, splashing this at the entrance of your house. Then place the package tied with ribbons into the coconut. Put the seeds, flakes, or powder in the coconut. Pour the herbal elixir in it. Then dash some of the perfume you wear into the hole. Seal it with the foil. Light the cigar. Puff smoke all over the coconut so it is enveloped in it. Now wrap the coconut tightly in your piece of clothing. Place the coconut on your altar.

Light one candle per day, and pray every day to Santa Muerte, asking her to improve relationships with your boss and petitioning for whatever you require from them. Keep the coconut in a safe place until Santa Muerte comes through for you, at which point, buy her a bouquet with yellow and blue flowers.

Spell for Prosperity in Any Aspect of Your Life

Ingredients:

white or blue plate

glass of water; the glass must be new

7 tablespoons of sugar

coin or bill

7 blue Santa Muerte candles

paper (white without lines)

On the plate, place the glass of water containing the seven tablespoons of sugar and the coin or bill; then place the seven blue candles around the glass. Write your petition of work, money, love, health, prosperity, or other on the piece of paper. Only one request is allowed on the paper.

Place the paper under the glass of water, saying the following prayer:

> *I invoke the heavenly court of divine and earthly justice,*
> > *of Santísima Muerte,*
> *So that these candles illuminate my Spiritual and Earthly paths.*

Pray one Our Father, one Hail Mary, and one Father, Be Glory; then make this statement out loud:

> *I (your name) am a successful, prosperous person who now joins others*
> > *who flourish.*

Leave the candles burning until they go out; then throw them away.

Spells for Health

Spell to Cure Someone Rapidly

Ingredients:

new white plate

1 handful of cornmeal flour

glass of Holy Water

pencil

piece of white paper

medium-sized crucifix

rosemary or rue herbs

1 Santa Muerte candle either white, purple, or of seven colors (siete
potencias)
wooden matches

On the plate, form a circle with the flour. In the middle of this, place the glass with Holy Water in it. With the pencil, write the name of the sick person on the paper; now place the paper underneath the glass, and on top of the glass, place the cross. Light the dried rue or rosemary, using it as incense, and purify the space you are working in as well as the plate and its contents. Light the white, purple or *siete potencias* candle with the wooden matches and say the following prayer:

> *O, great Lady of Light,*
> *I humbly ask you to give health and ward off disease from*
> *(person's name)*
> *So that well-being and spiritual strength can reach our home,*
> *Thank you, most Holy Lady, for listening to me.*

Place the candle next to the plate and let it burn constantly.

Once it's done, collect the flour from the plate and sprinkle it next to a tall, strong tree. Bury the paper below the tree and then sprinkle Holy Water in every corner of your house or the house of the afflicted person.

Spell to Restore Your Own Health

This spell will remove any disease or illness, natural or supernatural. This ritual is best performed on a Monday morning.

Ingredients:

rue, thyme, basil, and garlic
5 liters of water
1 white rose (you will need the petals)
alum stone
1 bar of Santa Muerte soap (jabon Santa Muerte)
1 purple Santa Muerte candle
white clothes

Boil the herbs and garlic in the water to make a strong herbal infusion. Put the petals and alum in the water. Take a bath or shower as usual. Then, if you have access to it, wash with Santa Muerte soap; then use the boiled mixture to rinse yourself (if the water is very cold, you can add hot water to warm it). In each application, as you rinse, visualize yourself with health and prosperity, and your body will be spiritually clean. Dress yourself in white clothes. Then take the candle and rub it over all of your body, especially the affected area. Light it. Pray to Santa Muerte:

> O Niña Blanca,
> Lady of Light and Peace,
> I humbly ask you to give me health,
> And rid me of disease.
> Bring back my well-being,
> And all pain decrease.
> Rid me of sickness
> And all infection release.
> Bring strength, both physical and spiritual,
> To my soul, body, and mind.
> O, Niña Blanca,
> This sickness I now leave behind.
> Amen.

Spell to Remove Curses Making Someone Ill

This spell is to remove curses and evil energies making you or a loved one sick.

Ingredients:

black marker

3 purple Santa Muerte candles

3 white candles

2 pieces of white paper

1 statue of Santa Muerte (purple or white ideally) from which you can
    remove her scythe

3 white cloths

1 bunch of epazote (use sage or rosemary if that is not available)
1 bunch of basil
1 bunch of chamomile
1 bunch of rue
1 photo of the sick person
coconut water
1 foot of white ribbon
Holy Death Powder (polvo Santa Muerte; or use yerba Santa Leaf in
*   polvo, also known as Hierba Santa Polvo and Hoja Santa polvo, or*
*   white clay if you cannot get this)*
copal, rue, or rosemary incense
1 egg
1 lemon
2 glasses of water
1 glass of tequila
3 purple or white flowers
2 images of Santa Muerte

Write the name of the sick person with your black marker on the glass of the purple candles or etch their full name in the wax. Do the same on the white candles. Write the name of the person on the two pieces of white paper, nine times on each paper, and list their health troubles.

On your altar, remove Santa Muerte's scythe and roll up the first piece of white paper and place it in her hand.

Take the second white sheet of paper, wrap it around the photo of the person, and place it in the center of one white cloth. Now place all the herbs on the wrapped photo, sprinkle some coconut water on the herbs, and then make a package of it all by gently closing this with the white ribbon within the white cloth so it forms a sort of pouch. Make sure it is not completely closed as you need to add an element to it later.

Take the *Polvo Santa Muerte* and make a circle on the floor. Have the sick person stand in the circle. Do not let the person exit the circle until cleansing is complete. Cleanse the person nine times from head to toe with incense, making sure to pass this over the top of their head, hands, belly, legs, buttocks, and so on. Then take the two remaining pieces of white cloth. Place the egg in one and the lemon in the other. Put one in each hand of the person.

Break the egg into a glass of water; then flush it down the toilet. Pour the lemon juice into a glass of water and have the person drink it.

Now take each unlit candle and pass it (not necessarily touching but close to them) over the person from head to toe. Take a sip of some tequila and spray it on the face of the person and their body and offer the rest to Santa Muerte. Take the three purple flowers and pass them over the body of the person from top to toe. Then offer the flowers to Santa Muerte. Next, take the two photos of Santa Muerte and pass them over the person from top to toe. Then untie the package with the white ribbon and the photo of the person inside, place one of the pictures of Santa Muerte in it, tie it up tightly with the ribbon, and place it on the altar. Now give the second picture to the person, who must keep it on themselves at all times.

Now pray for them:

> *Santa Muerte,*
> *O Mother of Illness,*
> *I come to ask you and I pray that you carry this harmful and negative*
> *   energy from the body of (person's name), so they have spiritual*
> *   and material health.*
> *My Lady, transform this energy and the offerings that I give to you,*
> *Into health and well-being for this person, and do not let disease*
> *   plague their body.*
> *Thank you, Mother of Disease and Death,*
> *For your divine intercession,*
> *Thank you for the cleansing, protection, and healing of (person's name).*
> *I place this in your hands and ask you to break and eliminate this hex*
> *   on (person's name).*
> *So be it, let it be so.*
> *Amen.*

The person is now cleansed and can step out of the circle.

Justice Spells

Penal Justice Spell

This spell will allow you to be freed of charges and ensure you are not incarcerated for your crimes. Do it two days prior to the first day of court or the first appearance before judges.

Ingredients:

large, fresh piece of wax paper or other thick paper
piece of palo justicia (these consist of sticks from the custard apple tree)
large Santa Muerte statue (ideally green, but other colors may be
    appropriate)
1 yard of green ribbon
1 new needle
1 green Santa Muerte candle of justice
1 small statue of Santa Muerte dressed in silver

Write your full name, the court action, case, or file number on the piece of paper. After this, place the piece of *palo justicia* and the image of Santa Muerte on the paper. Roll up the statue in the paper with the piece of *palo justicia* to make a packet, and seal it tightly with the green ribbon. With the needle, write the legal requests you wish for in the green candle wax.

Light the green candle and recite this prayer for justice:

> *Blessed Santa Muerte,*
> *Protector of the weak and helpless,*
> *Mother of Eternal Justice,*
> *Mistress of Wisdom,*
> *You who look into the hearts of the bad and the good,*
> *I approach you, Lady, to implore you for justice.*
> *To you, Santísima Muerte,*
> *I request the impartiality of your scales.*
> *My Lady, see my heart,*
> *Listen to my prayers that come out of need,*

Please, may justice be done on this earth,
May your divine hand guide the decisions of judges and jailors.
Powerful Lady,
Be ruthless with the wicked and backstabbers,
Be fair with the innocent
And benevolent with those who repent
Of heart and spirit.
O Santa Muerte,
Hear my prayers and protect me
Of iniquity and indolence.
On this day I request your favor
That my case be submitted for your consideration
And that I obtain absolute acquittal
Of all the earthly judges.
When the time comes, you will judge me,
And you will take the words that I have now pledged.
As the measure of my punishment or my absolution.
Amen.

Leave the spell work packet next to your statue and leave the candle burning. Leave the spell parcel for nine hours beside the large and small statues of Santa Muerte. After this, you must carry the spell packet in your pocket whenever you have a hearing or other dealings with the legal authorities related to your case.

Spell for Justice Against Someone Who Has Hurt You

Ingredients:

piece of white paper
black pencil
1 black Santa Muerte statue whose scythe you can remove
1 red rose
1 chocolate
1 glass of tequila/mezcal/other hard liquor

1 cigar

1 black marker

3 black Santa Muerte candles (make sure these are the ones that burn for
  7 days)

9 black candles (tall tapers)

You must say this prayer for nine days. This spell is very strong and will harm you if you are using it only for revenge, so you must be justified; otherwise, everything will return to you three times.

First, use the pencil to write on the white paper nine times the name of the person or the people who hurt you and caused you injustice or to go to jail or hurt your loved ones. Roll up the paper, remove la Niña Negra's scythe, and place the rolled-up paper in her hand. Thank her for helping with this spell; now place the Niña Negra back on her altar and give her the red rose, the chocolate, and the glass of tequila/mezcal/hard liquor. Light the cigar, cover her with the smoke, and then offer her the rest (place on her or by her in an ashtray). Now, using the black marker, write the name of the person whom you seek justice against three times on each of three Santa Muerte black candles so that in total it is written nine times, and then also etch it into the wax of the nine tapered or plain black candles. As you do this, focus all your hatred onto the candles.

Place in front of la Niña Negra. Light one black Santa Muerte candle and two tapered candles. Say this prayer:

> *Powerful Niña Negra*
> *Today I come before you,*
> *Seeking your justice.*
> *Merciful Lady,*
> *I ask you look upon me not as my judge but as my lawyer.*
> *I ask you, Niña Negra,*
> *Listen to my appeal*
> *And show me the power of your scythe for delivering rapid justice.*
> *This person (say the name of the person you want justice reaped upon*
>   *nine times)*
> *Injured and offended me and my loved ones.*

This problem is beyond my control,
And the law will not help me.
Only you can.
My Holy Mother,
Protect my home and my loved ones.
I ask you to torment and attack this vile person (say the name of the
    person nine times)
And anyone else who was involved in this action against me and my
    loved ones.
I pray you grant me justice.
I ask you to do (make petition) upon (say the name of the person
    nine times).
Let them suffer and feel your anger.
I ask you to inflict pain, suffering, and supernatural disease on this
    vile person (say the name of the person nine times).
I ask that nothing but bad luck and misfortune befall (say the name of
    person nine times) and anyone else who was involved in the harm
    of me and my loved ones.
Niña Negra,
My Queen, my Mother,
I beg you to deliver justice with speed and without compassion or pity
    on (say the name of the person nine times)
And on anyone else involved in this dirty business.
O Beloved Death of My Heart.
Be Ruthless with your scythe.
O, Santa Muerte.
Amen.

Each day, light a new black Santa Muerte candle and two tapers. Leave them burning during the nine days and, if necessary, thereafter.

Spell to Keep Vices Away and Beat Addictions

Ingredients:

1 amber Santa Muerte statue

white piece of paper (must not have lines or anything else)

13 blue candles (navy blue)

glass plate

3 white stones

lavender oil

eucalyptus oil

mint oil

olive oil

tree sap

Put the amber Santa Muerte statue on your altar. Write the name of the person on the piece of paper and on the wax of the 13 blue candles; then place the paper on the plate, then the candles, on top of the paper. Place the stones in a triangle with 13 drops of each oil on them on the paper, which should be sitting on the glass plate. Pour the sap on the candles. Place the plate before the amber Santa Muerte statue. When lighting the candles, make your request to the amber-colored Santa Muerte with great faith. This step should be done at night, preferably on Saturday. Then recite the following:

> *Holy Death,*
> *Queen of the Night,*
> *You for whom all is possible,*
> *With much humility, I implore you*
> *To heal (person's name) of their addictions and vices.*
> *With your powerful scythe, cut the addictions that afflict (person's name),*
> *Keep them from bad places, bad faces, and poisoned friendships*
> *That only bring sadness, sickness, and loss.*
> *Slice them away, make them fear you, Santa, and push them*
> *   elsewhere.*

O, Nina Blanca!
Only you are capable of making good upon this request.
Holy Death,
Sweet Lady of the Night,
Remove all obstacles and anything that would prevent (person's name)
From quitting their vices, drinking, smoking, drugs.
Slice them all away,
And I will be eternally grateful to you,
I will always adore you.
O Santísima Muerte.
Only you are capable of making this request,
So it is I turn to you for your great power.
Let it be so, O Holy Death.

Vinegar Spell against Addictions

If someone close to you is addicted to alcohol, drugs, pills, smoking, and so on, this spell will help them break their vices.

Ingredients:

rue
water
3 amber Santa Muerte candles
1 glass bottle with a lid (plastic will not work)
apple cider vinegar
drug, booze, etc., that the person consumes
tape
cotton ball

Boil the rue in water to make a sort of tea. Etch the addict's initials on the amber candle, then light the amber candle to Santa Muerte and ask her for help.

Take the glass bottle, fill it halfway with apple cider vinegar and the other half with the alcoholic drink, or place the drug that the person consumes in the vinegar. As you do this, recite with faith:

May this vice turn sour and bitter in your mouth.

Close the bottle and seal it totally with the adhesive tape. Then take the bottle again in your hands and, shaking it, repeat seven times:

While the bottle remains closed . . . you will not fall again into your addiction.

Before finishing, moisten a cotton ball in the rue water and clean the bottle with it. Then put it in a secret place out of the addict's reach.

Light the two other candles. Let them burn. Once they have burnt, throw the bottle into the waters of a river while concentrating on the prompt recovery of the afflicted person. If they have not recovered in three months, repeat the ritual.

Hexing Spell

This is a powerful spell to hurt your enemies. This spell is best done on a waning or moonless night.

Ingredients:

1 black (or dark red) rose
1 glass of tequila/mezcal/hard liquor
1 chocolate
1 cigarette or cigar or copal or mugwort incense
1 black Santa Muerte statue
3 Santa Muerte black candles
1 piece of rope, preferably black and made of leather, long enough to tie in knots
If possible, a photo or ideally something that belongs to the person you wish to hex (hair, clothing, etc.)

Go to your Santa Muerte altar and make your offerings of rose, a glass of alcohol, and chocolate. Also blow cigar, cigarette, or incense smoke over your Niña Negra. Light the nine black candles.

Now recite this prayer. As you say, "With this knot," tie each knot in the rope:

Niña Negra,
O, Santa Muerte
Hear my plea for justice
With this first knot seal this hexagonal deal
(name of your enemy) will not sleep,
(name of your enemy) will not rest
Knots of anger,
Knots of hatred,
Discord brings you (enemy's name) to your destination.
Niña Negra,
Hear my plea for revenge.
I tie this second knot,
And as I tie two,
Discord brings you (enemy's name) to your devastation
Niña Negra,
Hear my plea for domination
With this third knot,
And as I tie three,
Discord brings you (enemy's name) to deadly disaster,
Slander, discord, and evil too,
Bringing the darkness straight to you,
Weaving chaos in your mind
And total blackness on your path.
Hex of anger, hexagon of hate,
Finish (enemy's name) off, I won't wait,
So now make yourself manifest!
O Niña Negra!

Bury the rope with the photo or item of the person in a graveyard close to someone who died young or tragically.

Destruction/Confusion Spell

This spell brings destruction to an enemy. Please use this spell with care; it is powerful when done correctly. Ideally, this spell should be done during a waning moon or on a moonless night.

Ingredients:

pair of scissors

1 large dried chili (guajillo is a good choice; it has to be large enough to contain the photo)

1 picture of your enemy

black pen

1 packet polvo destruccion (destruction powder) or polvo confusion (confusion powder); it can be replaced with black salt or dog feces

1 needle

1 red piece of string or thread at least 20 inches long

1 small black Santa Muerte statue

1 black Santa Muerte candle (Muerte a mis enemigos; death to my enemies)

matches

Cut your chili down one side not quite to the edge, so as to make a pocket. Take the photo of your enemy, write on it the person's date of birth, name, and if you wish, all the bad things you wish to befall them. Sprinkle the powder on their face (*destruccion* if you want to destroy them, *confusion* powder if you just wish them to muddle up their affairs). If using salt, sprinkle this, or if dog feces, then mash it into their face. Next, fold the photo in half and then half again with the face on the inside, or fold it small enough so that it can fit into the chili. Put it in the chili. Seal the chili by putting a needle through its center. This must pierce both the chili and the photo. Then in the center, just by the needle, tie the red string around the chili; keep tying it around the chili until the entire length of the chili is tied with the string and is sealed tightly.

Place this chili by your small, black statue. Choose a hexing prayer from this book or create your own by humbly imploring Santa Muerte to bring whatever destruction or confusion you desire to the person's life. Etch the person's name and date of birth in the black candle. Light it with matches and focus all your hatred into the flame. Recite your prayer, focusing all your evil desires into the flame and chili. Let the candle burn completely; look at it and the chili often, focusing your intent into them. When the candle is fully burnt down, throw the chili and small black statue and candle remains in a dark, dirty place of bad energy, such as a ditch in a horrible area, a cesspool, a sewer, or a filthy, abandoned, dilapidated house with rats in it.

Ritual to Break a Spell

This spell can break another spell cast on you or one that you cast on another person, but you will need a piece of clothing, theirs or yours, to break it.

Ingredients:

1 personal garment
1 coconut
piece of paper
black pen
1 piece of black cloth
1 yard of black ribbon
rue water
1 pot (plant pot or other, must not be plastic; must be clay, steel, or other
   natural material)
herbs of basil, sage, and rosemary
water (as necessary)
Santa Muerte soap
white clothes
2 white Santa Muerte candles
wooden matches
1 cigar

Take the coconut water out of the coconut. Write your full name on the paper with the pen, roll up the paper, and place it within the black cloth. Then tie it with the black ribbon to form a packet. Make a hole in the coconut, place the packet inside, and then pour the rue water into it. Keep some rue water aside for later. Wrap the coconut in the garment to seal it. If the spell to be broken has been cast on you, very carefully pass the coconut repeatedly over your entire body. When finished, immediately put it in a pot and bury the pot well away from your house.

When you come back, boil the herbs in water for three minutes, strain them, and add a little rue water. Bathe with Santa Muerte soap; then upon your rinse, pour the mixture all over your body. Dress in white clothes. Light the candles with the matches and pray with great faith, asking Santa Muerte to free you from all kinds of malevolent magic work or to break the spell you have cast on another. Finally, light the cigar for Santa Muerte and thank her for the favors received. Perform the cleansing part of the rite as many times as deemed necessary.

❀ 💀 ❀

Unbonding with Santa Muerte: Ritual to Break Up with Death

I hate to place this ritual in a book dedicated to Most Holy Death, and for this reason, it is in a separate chapter, well away from everything else. Nevertheless, I am aware that some people, after having attempted to work with Santa Muerte, may decide the faith is not for them and, as such, may decide to "break up with" Santa Muerte, knowing that they will meet her fleshless, bony form upon their death when she comes to reap their soul. For this reason I include this ritual. The rite recommends you bury your Santa Muerte statue during a ceremony to her, but it is also acceptable to cleanse the items and then give them away to someone who is a true devotee and who willingly accepts them. They must, however, also then thoroughly cleanse the statue(s) and any other devotional items you give them.

Ingredients:

seeds
clay jug
jug with beer, tequila, mezcal, or other libation
white candle

Dig a hole that will contain your Santa Muerte statue(s) in the countryside or far away from your home in a tranquil spot. Explain to her that you need to part with her and accept that you will see her at the end of your time on earth. Put the seeds in the hole along with the jugs. Put the Santa Muerte statue(s) in the hole too, as upright as possible. Fill the hole with dirt. Light the candle and place it over the buried items, letting it burn completely. Walk away, and as you do, thank Santa Muerte for having entered into your life and tell her that you must part from her for now.

CHAPTER NINE

Santa Muerte's Birthday/ Deathday: Ritual of Celebration

Courtesy of Dr. Kate Kingsbury

The Day of the Dead, or *Dia de Muertos*, is celebrated on November 1 and 2. This is a time when Mexicans remember their dearly departed, honoring the deceased, in particular family members, keeping them and their bonds to them alive through memories and altars that they build to commemorate family members. Children are honored in processions and graveyards on November 1 on the *Dia de los Innocentes*, or *Dia de los Angelitos*, and adults on November 2. While some honor her during other times, such as the month of August, since Enriqueta Romero placed her effigy of Santa Muerte outside her home in Tepito on the Day of the Dead (and I even have heard before then), most Devotees of Death have chosen to honor Santa Muerte's Birthday or, more accurately, Deathday, during *Dia de Muertos*. This is a time to ask nothing of Santa Muerte and only pay homage to her. It is also a time to pay tribute to and connect with any ancestors and deceased relatives; you may call on them for advice/guidance or simply to reconnect.

In Mexico, while this is a time of remembrance, it is not somber. The funereal meets the festive. While there is nostalgia and sorrow, it combines with jollity and revelry, culminating in carousing! People dance, drink, and eat fine foods with their ancestors. Santa Muerte celebrations, while commencing on religious, mystical notes, soon soar into ecstatic parties where live bands fill the air with plangent ballads but also frenetic beats, and people dance with elan as drink flows freely through their veins, and marijuana may dizzy their brains!

I have devised this ritual to follow suit with what I have seen occur at some Santa Muerte chapels during the Day of the Dead, on October 31 or November 1, but feel free to adapt it to your desires. You should first cleanse your altar and statues thoroughly. Then, on the morning of November 2, sing "Happy Birthday," or play "Las Mañanitas" (a traditional Mexican birthday song that can be found online) to Santa Muerte. Lay a sumptuous spread of offerings on your altar fit for Queen Death. Adorn it with *papel picado* (perforated decorative paper) if you can get it. If possible, offerings should include *cempasuchil* (marigold flowers); foods such as candy, chocolate, honey, *pan de muerto* (bread of the dead), fruits; copal incense; sugar skulls; also optional is a cross. There should, of course, be water, and at this time, salt is now allowed. Give generous amounts of alcohol, whether it is hard liquor, such as tequila or mezcal, or beer. At the apex of the altar should be Santa Muerte herself, elevated above everything else. You may also place photos of deceased loved ones below Santa Muerte and gift them any foods, drinks, tobacco, or other items they particularly liked. If they died while children, place a toy or other child's item before them. Play music before the altar, for Santa Muerte and for your deceased relatives. Light candles for Santa Muerte and Day of the Dead candles if you can obtain them; they usually feature skulls, Catrinas, and other Mexican imagery. Light one white candle for each deceased relative or friend. You may also make a lavish meal and share plates of food with Santa Muerte and the deceased.

This is a time to thank Santa Muerte, using the prayer of thanks in this book or an ad hoc prayer of gratitude. This is also a moment to talk to your ancestors. Ask Santa Muerte to help you connect with dead family and friends. Once she has granted you this favor, talk to them, tell them your news. You may also ask for their spiritual blessings and guidance. You should contemplate your altar, your life, and theirs, and give great thanks to Mother Death, telling her you are ready when your time comes, to be embraced by her bony arms once and for all.

This ritual need not be a serious one, unless you feel called to create a mystical setting. Indeed, following in the footsteps of folk saint devotees in Mexico, you may well choose to have a fiesta, a party for Santa Muerte, whether throwing this with other devotees or enjoying the night in a delightful duo with you and her alone. On this night in Mexico, many chapels hold a rosary in the morning or afternoon, but later, the mood changes and huge parties are held in Santa Muerte's honor. Mariachi come to play in her honor. People drink, dance, and are merry as Santa Muerte watches on, the flames of candles also dancing and Santa Muerte's spirit with it. I invite you, dear reader, to share not only your sorrows, woes, and wishes with Santa Muerte but also during this party, your successes, joys, and moments of mystical merriment. Indeed, Death is with us through it all, no matter who we are, where we live, what we are doing, what we are feeling, or how we choose to live our life. And we will all finally end up in Death's arms.

A Postscript

This book must now draw to a close, dear reader. Santa Muerte *Azul*, as ever, sits on my desk guiding me beneath the flame of a purple candle as I, with faithful fingers, type these closing words. She has much more to share with you through me, her loyal conduit, but we are running out of pages; therefore, I leave you with a few pearls of her wisdom. She reminds you that your days on earth will not be forever and that one day she will come for you; therefore, treasure what and who you have now, and do not wait for tomorrow, when you might only have today. Be grateful for every day of life she gives you, every next breath she grants you, every morning you wake to live again, every night she lets you and your loved ones drift off into sweet, peaceful sleep. Pray to her with fervent faith so that her scythe not yet reap your soul or cut your beloved's thread of life quite yet and instead, that she wield it to stir up seeds of love, health, and wealth from the cosmic realms and help you harvest them into happiness. Respect her power, honor her name, and accept her skeletal embrace so that you are ready when your time comes to be united with her forever.

Acknowledgments

Special and heartfelt thanks to the many devotees, *curanderos,* and *bru-jos* in Mexico whose knowledge made this book possible. I keep some of their names private, honoring their right to secrecy. In particular, I would like to thank the other Pretty Girl who, under the full moon, works her power, A.B.A.V., you are my best friend in the world, and I am so grateful to you for being in my life with me on this path with dearest Death, Santa Muerte. You are strong, beautiful, spiritual, and I admire you deeply. I am grateful to you for opening up to me in a world where, at times, it felt nothing could be trusted and where nothing was clear. Indeed, I am grateful to you for so many things, from patiently answering my myriad questions and explaining stories unfolding before us in unimaginable ways to teaching me how to read the insect omens and conduct a *limpia con huevo,* to your calmness, kindness, and above all, your sincere friendship. I am grateful to you for putting up with my bad driving and for making me feel less scared on dark roads at night. I am grateful for a million other things that I have no room to write, but come what may, I hope your path becomes clearer and that soon you will know which road to tread, with who and when, and that on that journey you will create, live, and be all you have so wished for. Te quiero mucho.

Dearest E.M., none of this would have been possible without you. You, like an Angel of Death Herself, flew into my life so unexpectedly, glowing with the white light you always carry from within. In the darkness of that night we met, you also resonated with the strength of a Death Goddess thousands of years old. You have healed me, you have guided me, you have been a beacon to reach for, live for, to love. You have changed my life so completely, taught me without words but just through your very being how to be humble, graceful, spiritual, exceptional. We come from such different worlds, yet I feel such a deep, unbreakable bond to you that is beyond words. Te amo.

I also thank mi hermana Mar A. con todo mi corazon y mi alma, you are an extraordinary woman. Thank you for inviting me into your secret world of mysteries and letting me partake in the most beautiful rituals of my life with you that changed my life forever so I could never step back from Death's gaze. You taught me what strong women are, what they do, how hard they work; you made magic before me and let me witness your majesty in so doing. You have traveled through so much to rise like a phoenix of a *bruja* on Santa Muerte's moon to heal us, to heal me. You have given me protection and care, keeping me away from danger, both physically and spiritually. You are beautiful inside and out. Te adoro tanto.

"I thank from the bottom of my heart and with great humility, Doña Queta, the magnificent founder of the *Altar de la Santa Muerte in Tepito*, Mexico City. I am profoundly thankful to you for the protection and blessings that you bestowed upon me. Prayers for those I care for most in Mexico have been heard at your altar to Santa Muerte. Your powerful presence heals and raises. Your strength, resilience, and unpresuming grandeur are an inspiration. I am particularly grateful for a rosary you led during which you removed a dark shadow I had carried, returning my spirit to me when I most needed it. Gracias Doña Queta for gifting us, the children of Death, your vital soul as a guide and an altar of immense beauty where Santa Muerte grants far-reaching miracles."

I also wish to thank deeply and with much sisterly love Yuri Mendez for her patience, trust, strength, and support and for opening her chapel door wide to me with huge generosity. Thank you, Yuri, my dearest friend for standing for all that is right in this world at a time when I needed that most.

I also am deeply grateful to the ever mysterious and deep Soraya Arredondo Hernandez for teaching me not to fear the dark side but to embrace it, for when evil comes knocking at your door, it is not a time to run away but to face it with full force. Soraya you taught me, more than anyone, to love *la Niña Negra*.

Thanks also to Arely Vazquez for the heartfelt chats, for telling me about her relationship with the magnetic Enriqueta Vargas and for her honesty in sharing her experiences with Death Herself. Arely has been a pioneer in the United States and is the leader of the Santa Muerte group based in Queens, New York. For those interested, she holds services and also yearly celebrations, and her Facebook group, "Santa Muerte New York," which is open to all. Her dignity, discretion, and kindness have touched me.

Thanks also to Alejandra for your unwavering support and kindness; even when we faced negative forces, you never let me down. You showed me how to work with dreams and shared yours. I hope all your dreams will come true in your new life.

I am so grateful to Freddo for keeping me safe under his watch and sharing with me his hard work building his chapel from nothing. *Gracias hermano.* I hope you will be kept safe, and please, Santa Muerte, keep Freddo under your watch constantly in these difficult times.

Thanks to Ricardo V. for your belief in me and my work and for instilling in me the confidence I needed, and for the spiritual protection you offered me through Santa Muerte.

Also I thank Estefania for listening and keeping me calm when I worried about my path and those placing obstacles on it. You helped me see that those obstacles could just be stepped over.

Thanks are due to historian, religious studies professor, and author of the academic book *Devoted to Death: Santa Muerte, the Skeleton Saint.* Dr. Andrew Chesnut, who kindly provided for this book, some of his artistic photos from his website, *skeletonsaint.com,* which is dedicated to Santa Muerte news and stories. He spent much time editing this book with immense care, attention, and thought. I am very grateful to him for everything: his analytical reading of this book, noticing typos and unclear sentences, added clarity to the text.

Thanks also to Kathryn Sky-Peck at Red Wheel/Weiser who patiently listened to me and put in much work to turn the cover into an image both mystical and beautiful.

Thanks also to Jane Hagaman at Red Wheel/Weiser for her efficiency and aid in managing the editing process.

Acknowledgments

Big thanks to Judika Illes, whose guidance and intelligence as well as dedication to this book have proved an immense support. She has put up with me being off the grid for months at a time, patiently waiting for me to resurface so this book could emerge. She has championed me every step of the way; sine qua non this book would not be in the reader's hands. I cannot convey how professional yet exceptionally kind, astute, supportive, and positive she has been.

Also, many thanks to anthropologist Dr. Kate Kingsbury, who edited this book with utmost respect for its mysticism and the magic of Santa Muerte. I appreciate the photos she provided. Her insights on esoteric Santa Muerte knowledge were immensely useful, especially her expertise on Indigenous Holy Death practices, *brujeria*, and *curanderismo*.

Last of all, but most importantly and vitally, my deepest thanks and gratitude to the beautiful SANTA MUERTE, who has blessed my life infinitely with miracles and wonders of all kinds. She makes sure I have all I need; she keeps me safe, listens to me attentively, and teaches me lessons I will not forget. Santa Muerte, your deathly touch has taught me how to live again but also how to die metaphysically and be reborn again and again in your sacred power. I will forever walk in your light and shadow with each day of life you gift me, until finally you take my soul in your bony and holy embrace forever.

About the Author

Cressida Stone is a doctor of religious studies whose life mission has been to learn and record spiritual traditions from around the world. For over twenty-five years, she has traveled extensively in Africa, Asia, Europe, and Latin America, working closely with religious practitioners to learn a variety of spiritual traditions to find new ways of empowering herself and others through the medium of spirit. She has spent the last six years studying with Santa Muerte *curanderos* in Mexico. Find her @secretsofsantamuerte.

To Our Readers

Weiser Books, an imprint of Red Wheel/Weiser, publishes books across the entire spectrum of occult, esoteric, speculative, and New Age subjects. Our mission is to publish quality books that will make a difference in people's lives without advocating any one particular path or field of study. We value the integrity, originality, and depth of knowledge of our authors.

Our readers are our most important resource, and we appreciate your input, suggestions, and ideas about what you would like to see published.

Visit our website at *www.redwheelweiser.com*, where you can learn about our upcoming books and free downloads, and also find links to sign up for our newsletter and exclusive offers.

You can also contact us at *info@rwwbooks.com* or at

Red Wheel/Weiser, LLC
65 Parker Street, Suite 7
Newburyport, MA 01950